MORITO

MORITO

moritos

gilda 1.00

padrón peppers 4.00

jamón ibérico bellota 9.50

bread basket 2.50 harissa 1.50

olives 3.00 smoked almonds 2.50

quail's eggs with cumin & salt 2.50

fuet - catalan salami with pickle 3.50

beetroot borani with feta & walnuts 4.00

spiced lamb, aubergine, yoghurt & pine nuts 5.50

tortilla with potato, peppers & sweet onion 4.00

jamón & chicken croquetas 4.00

salt cod croquetas 4.00

SAM & SAM CLARK

CONTENTS

INTRODUCTION

As the little sister of Moro, Morito is the noisier, more rebellious sibling, eager to experiment and explore. Through our collection of tapas and mezze recipes you will be transported to both the present day hustle and bustle of London's Exmouth market and a Mediterranean country of our choice.

With this book we wanted to introduce you to two of our great loves: our varied and mad staff and the loyal, beating heart that is London's Clerkenwell. It is impossible to think how Sam and I could enjoy cooking without these two factors in our lives. We acknowledge, here and now, that we would be nothing without the people we work with who breathe life into what we do, and to this great city that supports us.

People talk about the atmosphere in Moro and Morito, 'that hits you like a wall of joy'. There must be some strange alchemy involved because it's impossible to analyse or copy. All we know is that we are grateful every day and these pages celebrate the special environment where the creativity begins.

First and foremost this book is here to help you eat and cook wonderful mezze and tapas. The unique atmosphere this brings to the table should be a part of everyone's life. There is something inherently joyful and social about eating in this way. Thousands of possible food combinations lie within this book, none of which is wrong as long as you are happy. Just follow a few basic rules about trying to shop seasonally while varying the colour, flavour and texture within the mix.

Different effects can be brought to a meal, depending on how you approach the timing. At Morito plates are placed on the table as they are ready. Usually bread, olives and cold things first, followed by the hot things one by one as ready. This drawn-out way of eating exaggerates the sense of anticipation and extends the pleasure. Alternatively, BAM! Everything can be placed on the table at once for both impact and beauty. Or somewhere in between, perhaps?

Hopefully when you become familiar with where the recipes come from you can play, eating solely Spanish food accompanied by fine sherries or perhaps just mezze plates, accompanied by a healthy glass of Turkish raki or arak from the Lebanon. Whichever way you choose to use this book, we believe there is great potential for you to produce many an evocative and memorable meal.

Sam and Sam Clark

BREAD

BREAD

Bread is a symbol and bread is a tool. A symbol of life itself, a means of sharing your life with others. A tool of the most primitive yet sensual nature, used to scoop up little morsels of food to the mouth. For Morito we made the decision not to use sourdough bread. We felt that the Moro sourdough was not suited to every type of food. Good chewy bread, without being too heavy: that was what we wanted. We developed this recipe to make excellent flatbreads and these, as well as bread rolls and some crunchy *picos* (Spanish breadsticks), make up the Morito bread basket.

FLATBREAD

Za'atar is the name of a wild herb indigenous to the Middle East that tastes somewhere in between thyme and savory and is believed to promote strength. In the Lebanon, a blend of dried za'atar, toasted sesame seeds and ground sumac berries is mixed with olive oil and spread on flatbread called man'oushe. Man'oushe hot off the grill, rolled and stuffed with tomato, cucumber, black olives and mint, was one of our culinary highlights of Beirut. If you can't get za'atar or sumac, we recommend a mixture of 6 parts sesame seeds to 1 part dried oregano and 1 part dried thyme.

> **Makes 10–15 flatbreads**
> 600ml tepid water
> 750g organic strong white bread flour (Shipton Mill or Doves Farm), plus extra for dusting
> 1 heaped teaspoon dried yeast
> 1 teaspoon fine sea salt
> 1 teaspoon sugar
> olive oil, for drizzling
> 1 tablespoon za'atar spice mix (page 280)

Put all the ingredients except the olive oil and za'atar in a bowl or food mixer with a dough hook. Thoroughly combine, then knead for 5 minutes, or more if working by hand, until the dough feels smooth and elastic. Let the dough rest for 5 minutes, then knead again for 3 minutes. Allow the dough to relax, covered, for about 30 minutes.

Sprinkle a clean surface with flour. Knead the dough in the bowl briefly one more time, then pinch off pieces of dough a little larger than a golf ball. Sprinkle more flour on top, flatten them slightly and roll each one into a thin disc (around 3mm thick) with a rolling pin.

At Morito we grill flatbreads over charcoal to give them a delicious smokiness. Simply drizzle one side of the rolled-out dough with a little

olive oil, sprinkle on a little za'atar, then transfer to a low to medium barbecue and grill each flatbread on both sides until slightly charred and puffed up in places. Otherwise, heat a large frying pan or griddle pan over a medium heat, add 1 teaspoon of oil to the pan and wipe off the excess with kitchen paper. Drizzle one side of each flatbread with a little olive oil, then sprinkle with the za'atar, and cook on both sides as before.

MORITO ROLLS

Morito rolls came about in an effort to replicate the delicious *molletes* most famously produced from a 200-year-old recipe in Antequera, in the province of Málaga. Their character is a moist chewy roll that is deliciously crunchy when toasted. Perfect for all our needs.

Makes 15-20 rolls
600ml tepid water
750g organic strong white bread flour (Shipton Mill or Doves Farm), plus extra for dusting
1 heaped teaspoon dried yeast
1 teaspoon fine sea salt
1 teaspoon sugar
a little olive oil, for the baking sheets

Put all the ingredients except the oil in a bowl or food mixer with a dough hook. Thoroughly combine, then knead for 5 minutes, or more if working by hand, until the dough feels smooth and elastic. Let the dough rest for 5 minutes, then knead again for 3 minutes. Cover the dough and place in the fridge for 1-2 hours to relax. This helps when you shape the rolls, as the dough is quite sticky. Line 2 or more baking sheets with lightly oiled baking parchment.

To form the rolls, first give the dough one more quick knead in the bowl. Then pinch off pieces of dough just larger than a golf ball and place on the baking sheets in rough roundish shapes (the dough is very forgiving). Leave them to rest for 30-45 minutes in a warm place, until they have doubled in size. Meanwhile preheat the oven to 200°C/400°F/Gas 6.

Bake the rolls for 10-12 minutes or until golden brown. Remove from the oven and transfer to a cooling rack.

These rolls freeze well if par-baked for 10 minutes at 180°C/350°F/Gas 4. To finish, defrost thoroughly, put in an oven preheated to 200°C/400°F/Gas 6 and cook for 5-10 minutes or until golden brown.

We cook the rolls in Moro's wood oven. To protect them from the harsh, dry air of the kitchen, whilst proving and to save space, we made a proving box that fits one hundred rolls snugly.

CHORIZO AND FENNEL SEED ROLLS

We ate this bread in Avila, the pulse-growing region north-west of Madrid.
Serve the rolls with a salad of cucumber, tomato, onion and olives.

Makes 15-20 rolls
1 quantity of Morito Rolls dough (page 12)
2 tablespoons olive oil, plus extra for the baking sheets
400g cooking chorizo, cut into small cubes, or slicing
   chorizo sliced into ribbons (page 281)
2 teaspoons fennel seeds, lightly crushed, plus extra for
   sprinkling on top

After the dough has proved in the fridge, heat the olive oil over a medium
heat and fry the chorizo pieces until they begin to crisp and caramelise.
Remove from the heat and leave to cool slightly, then add to the dough, along
with the oil in the pan and the crushed fennel seeds. Knead for 2-3 minutes;
the dough will become a lovely pink colour.

Pinch off pieces of dough just larger than a golf ball and shape them
into rough rounds. Place on 2 or more baking sheets lined with oiled baking
parchment and leave to prove for 30-40 minutes in a warm place, until they
have doubled in size. Bake as in the Morito Rolls recipe.

GREEN OLIVE AND WALNUT ROLLS

We first ate these stuffed breads on a family holiday in the Turkish city of Gaziantep, close to the Syrian border. One of our Morito chefs, Turguy, had invited us to his family home. We arrived to a table heaving with little plates of wonder and delicacy.

Makes 15-20 rolls
1 quantity of Morito Rolls dough (page 12)

STUFFING
230g green olives, pitted and roughly chopped
200g walnuts, roughly chopped
3 teaspoons coriander seeds, crushed, plus extra for
   sprinkling on top
1 small bunch of flat-leaf parsley, shredded
200ml extra virgin olive oil
juice of 2 small lemons
1 level tablespoon sugar

While the dough is proving in the fridge, mix all the stuffing ingredients together and season with a little salt and pepper.

To form each roll, place a piece of dough the size of a golf ball on one floured palm and flatten it. Put 1 tablespoon of the stuffing mixture in the centre and carefully fold the dough all around it to seal it in completely. Place the rolls, seam side down, on 2 or more baking sheets lined with lightly oiled baking parchment. Leave to prove and bake as in the Morito Rolls recipe.

If you find the idea of shaping, stuffing and cooking the rolls too daunting, this stuffing is good eaten alone with bread, flatbread or pitta.

SQUID INK ROLLS

You can find squid ink in a good fishmonger's, delicatessen, or online. The addition of the ink to the dough will give it an incredibly rich, black colour and play games with your mind, making you believe the bread has been burnt to a crisp! At Morito we serve these rolls with grilled peppers, squid, and Mojo Verde (page 158) or grilled leeks with anchovy and paprika butter. Delicious.

Makes 15-20 rolls
1 quantity of Morito Rolls dough (page 12) incorporating 2 tablespoons or 8 x 4g sachets squid (or cuttlefish) ink (page 281)

If you are using sachets of ink, soak them in boiling water for 1 minute to loosen them. Follow the method for making Morito Rolls, omitting the salt and adding the squid ink with the tepid water.

LEEK AND FETA GÖZLEME

Gözleme is a sort of Turkish calzone, and this is a variation of the classic spinach and cheese gözleme. Ideal with some kind of crunchy salad.

Makes 4 gözleme
½ quantity of Morito Rolls dough (page 12)
2 tablespoons olive oil, plus a little extra for frying
20g butter
2 large leeks, trimmed and thinly sliced
1 teaspoon Aleppo chilli flakes (page 280) or ½ teaspoon
  chilli powder
2 handfuls of fresh mint leaves, finely shredded
½ teaspoon freshly ground cumin
½ teaspoon dried oregano
100g feta cheese, cut into slices 7-8mm thick and crumbled
flour, for dusting

Make the dough by hand, as the amount is too small for a food mixer. Place in the fridge to prove for 1-2 hours.

Meanwhile, heat the olive oil and butter in a pan. Add the leeks and a pinch of salt and cook for 10 minutes over a medium heat, stirring regularly. Now add the chilli, mint, cumin and oregano. Reduce the heat and continue to cook for another 10 minutes, until the leeks are soft and sweet. Remove, cool slightly, then stir in the feta and taste.

Try to avoid rolling the dough ahead of time, as it will become soft and difficult to handle. If you want to prepare the gözleme in advance, it is better to cook them, then simply reheat when needed. Take the dough out of the fridge, and give it a quick knead with your fingertips. Dust the work surface and rolling pin with lots of flour. Pinch off a quarter of the dough and place it on the floured surface. Dust with more flour and gently start to roll into a thin circle about 15cm in diameter and 2-3mm thick.

Cover half of the circle with one-quarter of the stuffing and spread evenly, though not quite to the edges. Fold over the other half of the dough to cover the filling then seal the edges by pressing them together. Repeat with the remaining dough and stuffing.

Heat a large lightly oiled frying pan over a medium heat. Place one gözleme in the pan (or on a low barbecue) and cook for 3 minutes until mottled brown underneath, turn over and repeat on the other side. Remove and cover loosely with foil. Repeat with the remaining gözleme. Serve warm or at room temperature.

PARA
PICAR

PARA PICAR

'Para picar' literally means 'for picking', but the Spanish term sounds more charming. Nibbling plays an integral part in the eating habits of those who live around the Mediterranean. The name given to the 'ritual' may vary from country to country (tapas, mezze, antipasti, etc) but the core purpose of it is the same: enjoying the company of others with drinks, food and a gossip. It is a way of keeping the mind sane and nurturing the body. The following recipes are tapas or mezze in their simplest form, to accompany a glass of sherry, arak or raki.

MARINATED OLIVES

This olive marinade has its origins in the souks of Morocco: first-rate olives of varying shades, textures and sizes fragrantly spiced with harissa, orange, coriander and preserved lemon and piled high in ornate enamel bowls.

Serves 4-6

350g mixed olives in brine, arbequina, niçoise, gordal, kalamata, petit lucques (page 280)

5 pickled chillies (page 280), sliced into 1cm pieces

1 teaspoon coriander seeds

1 teaspoon fennel seeds

5 black peppercorns

1 garlic clove, thinly sliced

1 red chilli, seeds in and cut into 5mm slices

zest and juice of 1 orange

3 bay leaves, preferably fresh

1 tablespoon roughly chopped flat-leaf parsley

1 tablespoon Harissa (page 176) (optional)

1 tablespoon preserved lemon rind, roughly chopped (page 280)

4 tablespoons extra virgin olive oil

Drain the olives and rinse briefly under cold water. Drain thoroughly again. Place in a bowl with all the other ingredients, stir well and leave to marinate for at least a couple of hours, preferably longer. These olives will keep well in the fridge for 2-3 weeks, covered, without the parsley.

[para picar]

GREEN ALMONDS WITH SALT

In mid to late spring, Eastern Mediterranean grocers start to stock the much-loved green almonds, which are the immature nuts before the shell has developed. We use them for a few things at Morito: sliced thinly in salsas, pickled, or eaten in the classic way just with a little salt, as part of a mezze and perhaps with arak. Almond trees grow quite well in London, and I (Samuel) remember, aged ten, an Iranian friend picking a green almond off a tree and munching on it on the way to the swimming baths. He gave me one to try and it had a sour crunch like nothing I had ever tasted before. The almond tree is the most-loved tree in our garden, as we fill the house with its blossoming branches all through February and it still manages to produce lots of fruit in late spring. Luckily for us, the squirrels have not yet developed a taste for green almonds.

ICED ALMONDS WITH SALT

This mezze is crazy simple, yet a very useful way to introduce a wonderful crunch to the selection of food on the table. Soaking the almonds makes the texture similar to that of a green kernel eaten straight from the tree.

Serves 4
200g whole blanched almonds
4 ice cubes
Maldon salt or other flaky sea salt

Generously cover the almonds with cold water and place in the fridge overnight. When you're ready to eat, refresh the water and put the ice in the bowl. We recommend a sprinkling of salt on each almond before eating. They keep for a day or two in water in the fridge.

ROAST ALMONDS WITH PAPRIKA

Mature almonds are given greater complexity and nuttiness by being roasted
and doused with smoked paprika. However, for the first seven years of Moro we
struggled with roasting our own almonds, as the quality went up and down like
a yo-yo. Burning them was a far too common and soul-destroying occurrence.
Years have been added to our lives by buying Spanish roasted and salted
Marcona almonds. Delicious with fino or manzanilla sherry.

Serves 4
250g whole blanched almonds or roasted salted Marcona almonds
  (page 281)
1 teaspoon olive oil
1 teaspoon smoked sweet Spanish paprika (page 280)
1½ teaspoons Maldon sea salt, ground as fine as icing sugar

Preheat the oven to 150°C/300°F/Gas 2. If using blanched almonds, spread them
out on a baking tray and dry-roast in the top of the oven for 20-25 minutes
or until golden brown. Remove and stir in the olive oil, paprika and salt.
Return to the oven for another couple of minutes then leave to cool. If using
roasted Marcona almonds, heat in the oven for 5 minutes before adding the oil
and paprika, but no salt.

GREEN PLUMS

At the same time as the green
almonds start to emerge, so
do the small, sour green
plums adored by the Turkish
and Lebanese. Like green
almonds, they are dipped in
a little salt with every
bite and often adorn mezze
tables in the springtime.
If you have access to a plum
tree of any type, why not
pick some at this sour stage
for this savoury experience.

CRISPY CAPERS

Capers are the unopened flower buds of the Mediterranean's tough and spiky
caper bush, or *Capparis spinosa* in Latin. At the restaurant we also serve
pickled caper berries, the fruit of the plant, which is eaten like a
small gherkin. In Cyprus one can even buy jars stuffed with the pickled
stalks and leaves, complete with thorns similar to those on a rose bush.
This very simple tapa is a celebration of the caper's unique umami quality,
with a crunchiness only possible from frying an opening flower bud. Heaven on
their own or with thinly sliced raw fennel and, of course, fish.

Serves 4
200ml olive oil
3 tablespoons capers in brine (page 280), drained, rinsed and
squeezed to remove excess liquid

Heat the oil in a small saucepan over a medium heat. When the oil is hot but
not smoking, add the squeezed capers and fry until they are puffed up and
crisp. Don't let them get too dark or they will taste bitter. Remove the
capers with a slotted spoon and drain on kitchen paper, until cool.

HOMEMADE PICKLES

Pickling can be quick and easy. Pickles are essential to any mezze selection,
or with any dish that needs tang and a twang.

Serves 8 portions for 4 people
750ml dry white wine
250ml Moscatel vinegar (page 280) or white balsamic vinegar
   (if using ordinary white wine vinegar, add an extra
   ½ tablespoon sugar)
1 tablespoon sea salt
2 tablespoons sugar
6 red chillies, whole
1 tablespoon coriander seeds
3 bay leaves, preferably fresh
1 tablespoon honey (optional)
2 medium carrots (150g), sliced into discs 5mm thick
½ small cauliflower (300g), broken into small florets
7 garlic cloves, as young as possible (page 281), peeled
300g raw beetroot (optional as it changes the colour), sliced
   into half-moon discs 2–3mm thick
2 tablespoons olive oil

To prepare the pickling solution, place the wine, vinegar, salt, sugar,
chillies, coriander seeds, bay leaves and honey (if using) in a saucepan
and bring to the boil. Now add the carrots, cauliflower and garlic and simmer
for 6 minutes. They will still seem quite hard after this time but they will
continue to cook after you take them out of the pan. Remove with a slotted
spoon, along with the chillies, and place in a bowl. If using beetroot, add
it to the pickling solution and simmer for 6 minutes, then remove and place
in a separate bowl. Turn off the heat and cool the solution for 10 minutes.

   To finish the pickles, mix all the vegetables together, transfer
to a sterilised 2-litre Kilner jar and pour over the warm solution. Cool
completely, then pour the olive oil on top to seal. They will keep for
2-4 weeks in the fridge.

MORITO DUKKAH

Dukkah is an Egyptian condiment and spice mix. We are not quite sure how authentic ours is, but, boy, once you've made it, you will want it to be part of your life. For a dip, just mix the dukkah with a little olive, rapeseed or argan oil (page 280), but in general, it is most useful as the great transformer, brilliant on chicken, spinach, braised carrots, cauliflower or roast pumpkin.

Serves 4
50g sesame seeds
50g butter
1 teaspoon cumin seeds, roughly ground
2 teaspoons coriander seeds, roughly ground
80g roasted cashews, roughly crushed
⅓ teaspoon hot paprika (page 280), Aleppo chilli flakes
**   (page 280) or chilli powder**

In a dry saucepan, lightly toast the sesame seeds over a low to medium heat, stirring regularly until they begin to colour, then set aside. Melt the butter in another saucepan and cook for 1 minute or until it caramelises. Add the cumin and coriander seeds, stir for 2 minutes, then add the crushed cashews and toasted sesame. Reduce the heat and cook for another 2 minutes, stirring regularly. Finally, add the paprika or chilli and season with salt.

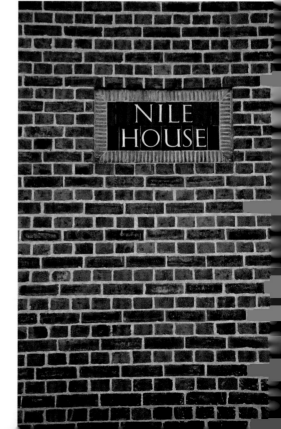

QUAIL'S EGGS, CUMIN AND SALT

School children in Morocco line up to buy hen's eggs with cumin, the ideal breakfast street food.

> **Serves 4**
> **2 teaspoons cumin seeds**
> **12 quail's eggs**
> **2 teaspoons Maldon salt or other flaky sea salt**

In a small frying pan, dry-roast the cumin seeds over a low to medium heat, stirring regularly, until they turn a shade darker and smell aromatic. Transfer to a mortar and pestle and roughly grind.

Bring a saucepan of water to the boil and carefully lower in the quail's eggs. Boil for 4 minutes, then remove from the water and cool under a running tap. In Morito we serve the eggs in their shells. Place on a small plate with the cumin and salt forming 2 small piles next to them.

[para picar]

CHERRY CHILLI PEPPERS, LABNEH AND PINE NUTS

We were recently introduced to a delicious type of sweet and spherical pickled red chilli, just right for stuffing. At Morito we use either labneh or Neal's Yard goat's curd for this mezze, but cream cheese also works well.

Serves 4
4 teaspoons pine nuts
8 teaspoons unspiced Labneh (page 91), goat's curd
    (page 281), or cream cheese with a squeeze of lemon
1 teaspoon za'atar (page 280) or ½ teaspoon dried mint
8 pickled cherry chillies (page 280), drained well
8 small mint leaves

Toast the pine nuts in a dry pan over a medium heat, stirring constantly, until they are speckled and light brown. Cool briefly before mixing 3½ teaspoons of them with the labneh, za'atar or mint and a pinch of salt and pepper. Using a teaspoon, fill each pepper with a decent amount of stuffing. Gently press the remaining pine nuts and the mint leaves on top of each chilli and enjoy!

PINCHOS

PINCHOS (PINTXOS)

In the Basque Country, you can find bar tops covered with a patchwork quilt of exquisite goodies known as pintxos. Similar delicacies may be found elsewhere in Spain but are called pinchos, montaditos or simply tapas and that is the beautiful contribution of language in creating identities. Pinchos are usually distinguishable from other small bites by having a wooden skewer through them; they may come with or without bread, which serves the dual purpose of keeping them together and making them easier to hold.

At Morito, we make a variety of pinchos throughout the year, depending on seasonality and mood. They tend to be the highlight of the eating experience, because more often than not they catch you by surprise. Their intense explosions of flavour and texture will definitely leave you smiling. We've included a few all-in-one-mouthful combinations, but allow your imagination to run wild. The main objective is to make simple and quick mouth-watering creations to fuel gatherings.

GILDA

Rita Hayworth's legs may seem a strange starting point for a pincho, yet this is how this popular tapita began: a pickled chilli, a green olive and an anchovy fillet on a cocktail stick, nicknamed Gilda after Rita Hayworth's legs in the 1946 film of the same name. A little bit unkind to Rita's legs, one has to say. We like the addition of a pickled silverskin onion popped on the end. The flavour is so intense: a bomb-blast that kick-starts your taste buds. We recommend having them on a hot day with a very cold beer.

Makes 8
8 guindillas or Turkish pickled chillies (page 280)
8 pitted green olives
8 best-quality (Ortiz) salted anchovy fillets (page 281)
8 pickled tiny silverskin onions

Assemble on the cocktail sticks as in the photo, but do keep them covered if you're not eating them immediately, as the anchovies will dry out.

ANCHOVY, TUNA AND OLIVE

Makes 8
8 best-quality (Ortiz) salted anchovy fillets (page 281)
8 bite-sized pieces of good-quality (Ortiz) canned tuna
   (page 281)
8 pitted green olives
4 guindillas or Turkish pickled chillies (page 280), halved
4 teaspoons Alioli (page 161), made without the garlic, or
   mayonnaise
¼ red onion, very finely chopped
1 tablespoon very finely shredded flat-leaf parsley

Wrap an anchovy around each piece of tuna and secure with a cocktail stick.
Add an olive at one end, and a half guindilla or pickled chilli at the other.
Finish with a tiny dollop of alioli or mayonnaise on the tuna, then sprinkle
the onion and parsley all over.

BOQUERÓN, CAPER BERRY AND PIQUILLO PEPPER

Makes 8
8 pickled caper berries (page 280)
8 boquerones (fresh anchovies cured in vinegar, page 281)
2 piquillo peppers (page 280), each cut into 4 strips
8 flat-leaf parsley leaves
extra virgin olive oil

Spike 1 of each ingredient on each cocktail stick then drizzle with a little
olive oil.

SQUID, CAPER BERRY AND TOMATO

Makes 8
16 x 3cm strips prepared and cooked squid (pages 198 and 200)
8 cherry tomatoes, cut in half
2 tablespoons extra virgin olive oil
1 tablespoon Forum Cabernet Sauvignon vinegar (page 280), or
   a good-quality aged red wine vinegar with a pinch of sugar
a handful of dill, chopped
8 pickled caper berries (page 281)

Toss the squid and the tomatoes with the olive oil, vinegar and dill and season with salt and pepper. Spike 2 pieces of squid and cherry tomato alternately on each cocktail stick and finish with a caper berry at one end.

OCTOPUS, POTATO AND GUINDILLA

Makes 8
16 x 2cm pieces of boiled (double-sucker) octopus (page 193)
3-4 boiled potatoes, cut into 16 cubes in total
8 pitted green olives
4 guindillas or Turkish pickled chillies (page 280), halved
extra virgin olive oil
smoked sweet Spanish paprika (page 280)

Spike 2 pieces of octopus and potato alternately on each cocktail stick and finish with a green olive at one end and half a guindilla at the other. Drizzle with a little olive oil, then sprinkle over some sea salt and the paprika.

mezze
tapas
raciones

PRAWN, ARTICHOKE AND JAMÓN

Makes 8
16 cooked prawns, peeled
2-4 fresh (cooked) or preserved artichokes, cut into 16
  wedges in total
16 small, thin slices of jamón (page 281)
extra virgin olive oil
a squeeze of lemon
a handful of flat-leaf parsley, chopped

Spike 2 prawns, 2 artichoke pieces and 2 slices of jamón alternately on each cocktail stick. Drizzle with a little olive oil and a squeeze of lemon, season with salt and pepper, then sprinkle over the parsley.

ASPARAGUS, JAMÓN AND QUAIL'S EGG

Makes 8
4 blanched asparagus spears, each cut into quarters
16 small, thin slices of jamón (page 281)
8 quail's eggs, hardboiled, peeled and cut in half
4 teaspoons Alioli (page 161), made without the garlic,
  or mayonnaise
extra virgin olive oil

Spike 2 pieces of asparagus, 2 slices of jamón and 2 quail's egg halves alternately on each cocktail stick. Finish with a tiny dollop of alioli or mayonnaise on the quail's eggs, drizzle with a little olive oil and season with salt.

MONTADITOS

MONTADITOS

The word montadito comes from the Spanish *montar*, which means to climb or assemble. In culinary terms, a montadito is similar to what the Italians call bruschetta, the main difference being that rolls tend to be used instead of bread. If you have no time to make Morito Rolls (page 12) or can't find crusty rolls you like, then two roughly 9cm x 6cm pieces of ciabatta, cut in half horizontally, are a good alternative. Montaditos can be changed into a *boccadillo* (sandwich) by adding an extra piece of bread on top. Indeed, one of our favourites for breakfast is a tortilla boccadillo with a fried green pepper.

PAN CON TOMATE (TOMATO TOAST)

Spain's iconic breakfast.

Serves 4
2 Morito Rolls (page 12),
   cut in half (or 4 pieces
   ciabatta)
½ garlic clove
4 heaped tablespoons finely
   chopped or grated ripe
   tomato
4 teaspoons fruity extra
   virgin olive oil

Lightly toast the rolls. Rub gently with the garlic and spread a tablespoon of the tomato on top of each toast. Drizzle generously with the olive oil and season with salt. Eat immediately.

PAN CON TOMATE CON JAMÓN (TOMATO TOAST WITH JAMÓN)

It is important to source good-quality acorn-fed jamón like ibérico de bellota (page 281). Make the tomato toasts as described opposite and top each one with thin but generous slices of jamón. A fried padrón pepper or two (page 280) or a pickled chilli (page 280) is a fitting addition.

Brief jamón knowledge
• Jamón serrano: a normal breed of pig that is salted, cured and hung to dry. It makes up over 80 per cent of the ham sold in Spain.
• Jamón ibérico and pata negra: refers to the semi-wild breed of iberian pig with its famous black hoof but, of course, it is how they are fed that is the key. If it says 'jamón ibérico de cebo' it is purely grain-fed.
• Jamón ibérico de recebo: free-range pata negras that eat a minimum of 50 per cent acorns, as well as a mixture of grains. It is the category that we use in Moro and Morito. Recommended by a friend, we visited the producer in the province of Salamanca, and have been buying their hams directly ever since.
• Jamón ibérico de bellota: this tells you it has been fed on 100 per cent wild acorns (*bellota*) and the meat aged slowly for at least three years.

QUAIL'S EGG AND JAMÓN

I (Samantha) had this tapa in a tiny bar in Granada on my first trip to Spain, with my great friend Lidia. We were visiting her brother David who was at the university. Being a foodie, he knew all the best bars, and we were blown away by the food and the atmosphere. Having coincidentally spent many years in France and Italy as children, Samuel and I both came to Spain relatively late but immediately fell in love with the country and made up for lost time.

> **Serves 4**
> **2 Morito Rolls (page 12), cut in half (or 4 pieces ciabatta)**
> **7 teaspoons extra virgin olive oil**
> **4 quail's eggs**
> **½ garlic clove**
> **4 heaped tablespoons finely chopped or grated ripe tomato**
> **4 thin slices of jamón ibérico (around 60g) (pages 49 and 281)**
> **a little roughly ground cumin**

Lightly toast the rolls. Meanwhile, heat a non-stick frying pan over a high heat and add 3 teaspoons of the olive oil. Quail's eggs are quite tricky to crack, so gently cut into them using a serrated knife, break them open (one by one) into a small dish, then slide them into the pan. They literally take about a minute to cook. Carefully remove with a spatula.

When the toast is ready, rub gently with the garlic and spoon over the tomato. Drizzle generously with the remaining 4 teaspoons of olive oil and season with salt. Top with the jamón, followed by the fried eggs and a tiny sprinkle of cumin and salt.

SERRANITO (LOMO, JAMÓN AND GREEN PEPPER)

A lomo (pork) montadito is a stalwart on any tapas menu, usually served on its own on bread or with chopped tomato and a fried green pepper. The addition of jamón changes the name of this tapa to a serranito, as it is more often found in the sierra (countryside), with both the jamón and pork from the ibérico (black-foot) pig. At Morito we use fillet because it is the most tender. Usually it's bought whole and weighs 250-400g. If you do not finish it in one go, the remainder can always be frozen.

Serves 4
8 teaspoons extra virgin olive oil
2 long green peppers or 12 padrón or frigitelli peppers
  (page 280)
160g pork fillet (tenderloin), cut into 8 slices 5mm thick
1 teaspoon fennel seeds, lightly crushed (optional)
2 Morito Rolls (page 12), cut in half (or 4 pieces ciabatta)
½ garlic clove
2 heaped tablespoons finely chopped or grated ripe tomato
4 very thin slices of jamón ibérico (around 60g) (pages 49
  and 281)

In a frying pan, heat 3 teaspoons of the olive oil over a medium heat. Add the peppers, season lightly with salt and pepper and fry for a couple of minutes on either side until blistered and just soft, but not dark. Remove from the heat, cut the long peppers in half, deseed (leaving the padrón or frigitelli peppers whole) and dab on kitchen paper to remove any excess oil. Keep warm. Wipe the pan clean and return to a high heat. Rub the pork slices with the fennel seeds, if using, season, then drizzle with 2 more teaspoons of olive oil. When the pan is hot, fry the pork for less than a minute on either side, until just cooked through and juicy. Remove from the pan and keep warm.

To assemble, lightly toast the rolls, rub gently with the garlic, then spread the tomato on top. Drizzle over the remaining olive oil. Add the jamón followed by the pork slices and finish with the peppers. Serve immediately.

ANCHOVY, TWO WAYS

This is a slightly larger tapa, as everyone gets one tomato and one avocado montadito. The contrast between the two creates one of the best pairings of flavours you will ever taste, preferably consumed in alternate bites.

Serves 4

TOMATO AND ANCHOVY

2 Morito Rolls (page 12), cut in half (or 4 pieces ciabatta)
½ garlic clove
4 heaped tablespoons finely chopped or grated ripe tomato
4 teaspoons extra virgin olive oil
4 best-quality (Ortiz) salted anchovy fillets (page 281)
1 green chilli, deseeded and chopped

Lightly toast the rolls, rub gently with the garlic and spread the tomato on top. Drizzle with the olive oil and season with salt. Place the anchovy fillets on top and sprinkle with the chopped chilli. Serve immediately.

AVOCADO AND ANCHOVY

1 large, ripe avocado
a squeeze of lemon
2 tablespoons extra virgin olive oil
2 Morito Rolls (page 12), cut in half (or 4 pieces ciabatta)
½ garlic clove
4 best-quality (Ortiz) salted anchovy fillets (page 281)
1 green chilli, deseeded and chopped

Peel the avocado and cut into thin slices. Place in a bowl with the lemon juice and olive oil and season.

Lightly toast the rolls and gently rub with the garlic. Arrange the avocado slices on top, followed by the anchovy fillets, then sprinkle with the chopped chilli.

MATRIMONIO

Another favourite anchovy montadito is called a matrimonio, literally the 'marriage' of one salted anchovy *anchoa* and one marinated anchovy *boquerón*. Very simple but utterly delicious.

Serves 4
2 Morito Rolls (page 12), cut in half (or 4 pieces ciabatta)
½ garlic clove
4 teaspoons extra virgin olive oil or 4 knobs of butter
4 best-quality (Ortiz) salted anchovy fillets (page 281)
4 best-quality boquerones (page 281)
1 tablespoon finely chopped flat-leaf parsley
zest of ¼ lemon

Lightly toast the rolls, rub gently with the garlic and then drizzle with the olive oil or spread with the butter. Lay the salted anchovies and boquerones side by side on the toast and finish with the parsley and lemon zest. Eat immediately.

OLOROSO CRAB

Chris Cooke, a friend and an excellent cook, showed us this delicious montadito made with crab from his local fish market in Jerez. The Oloroso sherry gives the crab a savoury richness and perfume. At Morito we cook and pick our own crabs and include a little of the brown meat, which makes the dish sweeter and more luscious. Crab montadito is a favourite at the Morito seafood festival held every September.

Serves 4
3 tablespoons olive oil
3 spring onions, thinly sliced, including the green part
1 garlic clove, chopped
1 teaspoon chopped thyme
6 cherry tomatoes, finely diced
⅓–½ teaspoon finely chopped deseeded red chilli
3 tablespoons Oloroso sherry (page 281)
1 tablespoon water (omit if using brown crab meat)
50g brown crab meat (optional)
1 tablespoon roughly chopped flat-leaf parsley
250g white crab meat, picked through for any shell
2 Morito Rolls (page 12), cut in half (or 4 pieces ciabatta)

Heat 2 tablespoons of the olive oil in a small saucepan over a medium heat. Add the spring onions, garlic and thyme and cook for 3 minutes, until softened, stirring every now and then. Add the tomatoes and chilli and cook for a further 3 minutes, then add the Oloroso. Simmer for 30 seconds before adding the tablespoon of water or brown meat and the parsley. Stir in the white crab meat and heat gently. Check the seasoning and stir in the remaining tablespoon of olive oil.

Lightly toast the rolls and spoon the warm crab on top.

SALT COD BRANDADA AND TOMATO

Think of brandada as a warm salt cod, potato and olive oil pâté. Roasting transforms even the most lacklustre tomato into something sumptuous. If you want to use smoked haddock instead of salt cod, obviously it will not be necessary to soak the fish but you will need to simmer it for a minute longer.

Serves 4
8 sweet cherry tomatoes
5-6 tablespoons extra virgin olive oil
a pinch of sugar (optional)
250g medium-cured salt cod fillet (page 281), soaked in cold water overnight (or 350g smoked haddock)
1 litre whole milk
3 bay leaves, preferably fresh
½ white onion, cut in half
350g potatoes, peeled and quartered
½ garlic clove, crushed to a paste with ½ teaspoon salt
2 Morito Rolls (page 12), cut in half (or 4 pieces ciabatta)
1 tablespoon roughly chopped flat-leaf parsley

Preheat the oven to 200°C/400°F/Gas 6. Mix the cherry tomatoes with 2 tablespoons of the olive oil, some salt and pepper and the pinch of sugar if the tomatoes are not particularly sweet. Spread the tomatoes out on a baking tray and roast for 20-30 minutes, until they begin to soften and are slightly charred. Remove and set aside.

Meanwhile, place the salt cod, milk, bay leaves and onion in a saucepan over a gentle heat. Just before the milk comes to a gentle simmer, remove the fish from the pot and add the potatoes. Make sure the potatoes are covered by the milk; if not, top up with water.

Meanwhile, shred the salt cod while it is still warm, removing the skin and any bones. Once the potatoes are tender, drain and retain the milk infusion. Transfer them to a bowl and mash. Add the salt cod to the potato mixture along with the garlic and the remaining olive oil. Mix everything together really well until it resembles soft mashed potato. If the mixture is too thick you can add some of the milk infusion and more olive oil.

To assemble, lightly toast the rolls and squash one cherry tomato on to each piece. Cover with a spoonful of brandada (we like it slightly warm) and place another cherry tomato on top. Drizzle with some of the tomato juices from the baking tray, sprinkle with the parsley and serve.

CHORIZO AND PIQUILLO PEPPER

We are very particular about our choice of cooking chorizo. The wonderful Brindisa supplies us with chorizo dulce from Catalunya that is pretty hard to beat, but a good (preferably ibérico) slicing chorizo is also delicious. Mojo verde, a fragrant green chilli sauce from the Canary Islands, gives this montadito a nice kick.

Serves 4

120g piquillo peppers (page 280), or 2 Romano peppers
  (page 280), grilled or roasted, peeled and deseeded
1 garlic clove, cut in half
1 sprig of thyme, leaves only
1-2 teaspoons Forum Cabernet Sauvignon vinegar (page 280), or
  a good-quality aged red wine vinegar with a pinch of sugar
1 tablespoon finely shredded flat-leaf parsley
8 teaspoons extra virgin olive oil
2 cooking chorizo (about 150g) (page 281), cut in half
  lengthways and each half cut into 2cm pieces, or slicing
  chorizo (page 281)
2 Morito Rolls (page 12), cut in half (or 4 pieces ciabatta)
2 heaped tablespoons finely chopped or grated ripe tomato
½ quantity of Mojo Verde (page 158), or 1 tablespoon shredded
  flat-leaf parsley

Thinly slice the peppers and one half of the garlic clove, and put in a bowl with the thyme, vinegar, parsley, 2 teaspoons of the olive oil and a pinch of salt. Leave to marinate.

Meanwhile, heat a frying pan over a medium heat, add 2 teaspoons of the olive oil and cook the chorizo on both sides until coloured. Keep warm.

Lightly toast the rolls and gently rub with the remaining garlic half. Spoon the tomato on top, followed by the remaining olive oil, then add a touch of salt and a few strips of pepper. Finish with the chorizo and a spoon of mojo verde or parsley. Serve immediately.

PICOS CHEESE, ANCHOVY AND JAMÓN

Blue cheese, salted anchovy and jamón may sound like the strangest of combinations, but it does work, creating a flavour explosion. Blue cheese and walnuts is a classic variation, served on toast or on a chicory leaf.

Serves 4
2 Morito Rolls (page 12), cut in half (or 4 pieces ciabatta)
½ garlic clove
4 teaspoons extra virgin olive oil
4 very thin slices of jamón ibérico (around 60g) (pages 49 and 281)
100g blue cheese (Picos de Europa (page 281), or Roquefort), thinly sliced
4 best-quality (Ortiz) salted anchovy fillets (page 281)

Lightly toast the rolls. Rub gently with the garlic and drizzle with the olive oil. Place the jamón on each toast followed by the blue cheese and anchovies. No salt needed!

MORCILLA AND GREEN PEPPER

There is something about fresh, juicy pepper combined with crisp morcilla (Spanish blood sausage) that makes this tapita irresistible. These peppers, available from Turkish greengrocers, are sweet, long and green and look like large chillies. Padrón, frigitelli or red Romano peppers also work well.

Serves 4
2 long, pointy green peppers, or 12 padrón peppers (page 280)
6 tablespoons extra virgin olive oil
1-2 teaspoons Forum Cabernet Sauvignon vinegar (page 280), or
    a good-quality aged red wine vinegar with a pinch of sugar
a pinch of freshly ground fennel seeds or cumin seeds
160-200g morcilla (page 281), or black pudding, cut into 1cm-
    thick slices
2 Morito Rolls (page 12), cut in half (or 4 pieces ciabatta)
½ garlic clove
1 tablespoon finely shredded flat-leaf parsley

If using long peppers, make a small slit in each one, just large enough to deposit a decent pinch of salt inside. Give the peppers a good shake. If using padrón peppers, keep whole and sprinkle with salt. Heat 3 tablespoons of the olive oil in a pan over a low to medium heat, add the peppers and fry until soft and lightly coloured on both sides. Remove the stalks and any seeds from the long peppers and cut each one in half (keep the padrón or frigitelli whole). Toss with the vinegar, fennel or cumin, set aside and keep warm.

In another pan, fry the morcilla or black pudding with the remaining 3 tablespoons of olive oil over a medium heat until crisp on both sides.

Meanwhile, lightly toast the bread, and gently rub with the garlic. Taste the juices in the pan. If they are sweet and fragrant, spoon them on to the toast (if not, drizzle the toast with a little extra olive oil). Top with the peppers and hot morcilla or black pudding and finish with the parsley.

FLATBREAD, LIVER AND CUMIN

A flatbread has snuck its way into the montaditos chapter, but it is a delicious snack that we ate on Green Lanes, in one of Haringey's many excellent Turkish establishments.

Serves 4
150g calf's liver, cut into bite-sized pieces
1 teaspoon cumin seeds, lightly toasted and ground (page 34)
½ small red onion, thinly sliced
1 tablespoon Forum Cabernet Sauvignon vinegar (page 280), or
   a good-quality aged red wine vinegar with a pinch of sugar
40g butter
a squeeze of lemon
1 large Flatbread (page 10) or pitta bread
1 tablespoon shredded mint or parsley leaves
½ teaspoon Aleppo chilli flakes (page 280), hot paprika
   (page 280), or chopped fresh deseeded red chilli

Season the liver with salt, pepper and half the cumin. Place the onion in a bowl, add the vinegar and a pinch of salt and leave to marinate a little. To cook the liver, place a pan over a medium to high heat and, when hot, add the butter, followed by the liver. Fry on all sides for 3-5 minutes, until golden brown on the outside, juicy and pink inside. Finish with a squeeze of lemon and leave to rest for a minute.

Lightly toast or grill the flatbread or pitta bread and cut it into quarters. Place the pieces of bread on a plate, lay the liver on top and pour over any juices from the pan. Sprinkle the onion over the liver, followed by the mint or parsley, the remaining cumin and the chilli.

EGGS AND DAIRY

Eggs

We had the strangest experience when we visited our egg supplier. We were chatting with the farmer, asking such questions as 'Can I see what the chickens are fed on?' and 'How fresh can we expect the eggs to be?', when he unexpectedly opened a side-door in his office, directly on to his barn where lots of chickens were waddling around. He said, 'Put out your hand', and a hen promptly laid a warm egg into Samuel's palm. Although comical, we found the moment surprisingly touching. Now, with each tortilla we make, we can't help but think of the miracle each egg represents.

HUEVOS ROTOS

Weekend brunch at Morito usually starts with huevos rotos – a chorizo, potato, onion and egg hotchpotch. This is a dish for workers, walkers or teenagers. It is heavy, but very authentic and delicious.

Serves 4
2 medium potatoes (225-250g), peeled and cut into 1cm cubes
4 tablespoons olive oil
100g cooking or slicing chorizo (page 281), sliced (optional)
1 Spanish onion, chopped
1 small red pepper, chopped
1 small green pepper, chopped
1 sprig of thyme
1 teaspoon finely chopped rosemary
1 garlic clove, finely chopped
4 organic or free-range eggs
1 tablespoon roughly chopped flat-leaf parsley
a sprinkling of smoked sweet Spanish paprika (page 280)

Add a generous pinch of salt to the cubed potatoes, toss well and leave in a colander for 15 minutes. Meanwhile, pour the oil into a large frying pan, add the chorizo (if using) and cook over a medium heat for a few minutes until it caramelises. Remove the chorizo and set aside. Now add the onion, peppers, thyme, rosemary and a pinch of salt to the pan. Cook gently for about 10 minutes, stirring occasionally, until the onion and peppers begin to soften. Stir in the potatoes and garlic and cook for another 15 minutes or until the potatoes are soft and tender but not coloured, stirring every now and then. Return the chorizo to the pan and crack the eggs into the mixture. Remove from the heat and gently mix everything together until the egg is cooked, returning the pan to the heat if necessary. Check for seasoning, sprinkle with the parsley and paprika and serve immediately, with bread or toast.

RED PEPPER TORTILLA

Red peppers add sweetness and colour to a tortilla. Perfect with a Gilda (page 38) and a glass of fino sherry.

Serves 6-8

2 medium potatoes (225-250g), peeled, sliced into quarters lengthways and cut into thin triangles

8 tablespoons olive oil

1 large Spanish onion or 2 medium onions, thinly sliced

2 sprigs of thyme

2 bay leaves, preferably fresh

2 red bell peppers or 3 Romano peppers (page 280), deseeded and sliced

¼ teaspoon sweet smoked Spanish paprika (page 280)

8 organic or free-range eggs

Toss the potatoes with ½ a teaspoon of salt, transfer to a colander and leave to stand for 15 minutes. Set a large non-stick frying pan over a medium heat and add 4 tablespoons of the olive oil. When hot, add the onion, thyme, bay leaves and a pinch of salt and cook for 10 minutes, stirring occasionally, until the onion is soft and golden. Add the peppers and paprika and continue to cook for 10 minutes until the peppers start to soften. Now add the potatoes and cook for a further 15 minutes or until tender but not coloured, stirring every now and then. Remove from the heat and transfer the mixture to a dish, discarding any excess oil. Cool for 5 minutes.

Crack the eggs into a large bowl and whisk lightly. Remove the thyme and bay leaves and fold the vegetable mixture into the eggs and check the seasoning. Wipe the frying pan clean and return it to a medium to high heat. When hot add 2 more tablespoons of oil and swirl it around the pan and up the sides to coat. As the oil begins to smoke, pour in the mixture, while gently shaking the pan with the other hand to ensure it is evenly spread. Lower the heat and let the tortilla cook for 3-5 minutes. Using a spatula, gently check whether the underside of the tortilla is golden brown and the runny exposed side has formed a ring of cooked egg around the edge. Remove from the heat, rest for a minute, then take a plate about the same size as the pan and rest it over the pan. Carefully invert the tortilla on to the plate. Return the pan to the heat. When hot, add the remaining 2 tablespoons of oil and gently slide the tortilla back into the pan to cook the other side. Lower the heat and tuck in the edges of the tortilla to neaten. Cook until golden brown underneath and firm to the touch, turning again if the tortilla is still runny in the middle. Remove from the heat and leave for a few minutes to settle, then turn the tortilla out on to a clean plate. Serve slightly warm or at room temperature.

SPINACH AND JAMÓN TORTILLA

Wild garlic leaves are widely available to forage for in British woodland
from early spring and make an excellent alternative to spinach in this
recipe.

Serves 6
25g butter
6 tablespoons olive oil
500g spinach or 300g wild garlic leaves, washed and drained
6 organic or free-range eggs
a pinch of dried oregano
100g jamón (page 281), finely chopped (optional)

Heat the butter and 2 tablespoons of the olive oil in a pan over a medium
heat. Add the spinach or wild garlic, season with salt and pepper and cook
gently for a couple of minutes until soft, stirring occasionally. Remove from
the pan, cool slightly, then gently squeeze to get rid of any excess water.
Place on a board, chop roughly and transfer to a bowl. Crack the eggs into
the bowl and gently mix together along with the oregano and jamón, if using.
Check the seasoning.

Place a large frying pan over a medium to high heat. When hot, add
2 more tablespoons of oil and swirl it around the pan and up the sides to
coat. Cook in exactly the same way as the Red Pepper Tortilla (page 72),
using the remaining 2 tablespoons of olive oil.

CRISP TORTILLA

At Morito we are quite particular about the crisps we use for this tortilla, preferring the delicate Spanish crisps cooked in olive oil. We buy ours from La Fromagerie, the wonderful cheese shop with branches in Highbury and Marylebone in London, but you will be able to find similar crisps in speciality food shops. This recipe is a variation on one in Ferran Adrià's brilliant book *The Family Meal* (Phaidon Press, 2011), which documents the staff meals at elBulli.

Serves 4-6
7 tablespoons olive oil
300g wild garlic leaves (if available), or 2 tablespoons chopped chives
6 organic or free-range eggs
190g packet of Spanish crisps cooked in olive oil, such as San Nicasio (page 281)

Place a pan over a medium heat, pour in 3 tablespoons of the olive oil and, when hot, add the garlic leaves (chives do not require any cooking). Season with a pinch of salt and cook for a few minutes, stirring occasionally, until soft and wilted. Remove from the heat, allow to cool, then squeeze the leaves to get rid of any excess liquid and chop roughly.

Crack the eggs into a bowl and whisk for a good 5 minutes, until pale and very frothy; this can be done with an electric whisk for a faster and fluffier result. Heat a large, non-stick frying pan over a medium to high heat. Add the crisps and the chopped garlic leaves or raw chives to the eggs, season with a little salt and pepper and mix. When the pan is hot, add 2 more tablespoons of oil and swirl it around the pan and up the sides to coat. Cook in exactly the same way as the Red Pepper Tortilla (page 72), using the remaining 2 tablespoons of olive oil.

SPRING VEGETABLE KUKU

Below is a recipe for *kuku, an* Iranian omelette.

> **Serves 6-8**
> 9 tablespoons olive oil
> 3 spring onions, thinly sliced, including the green part
> 1 bunch of asparagus (around 10 spears), trimmed and each
>   spear cut into quarters
> 1 large handful of podded fresh peas
> 1 large handful of podded and peeled fresh broad beans
> 1 small bunch of dill, roughly chopped, plus extra to serve
> 1 small bunch of mint, shredded
> finely grated zest of ½ orange
> 6 organic or free-range eggs
> 15 threads of saffron, steeped in 3 tablespoons boiling water
> 4 tablespoons unspiced Labneh (page 91), or 50:50 Greek
>   yoghurt and cream cheese

Place a large, non-stick frying pan over a medium heat and add 5 tablespoons of the olive oil. When hot, add the spring onions, asparagus, peas, broad beans and a good pinch of salt and cook gently for about 10 minutes, stirring often, until tender. Add the dill, mint and half the orange zest, mix well, then remove from the heat. Drain off any excess oil and cool slightly. Lightly beat the eggs in a bowl, stir in the vegetables, and the saffron-infused water, and check the seasoning.

    Wipe the frying pan clean and return it to a medium to high heat. When hot, add 2 tablespoons of oil and swirl it around the pan and up the sides to coat. Cook in exactly the same way as the Red Pepper Tortilla (page 72), using the remaining 2 tablespoons of olive oil. Serve slightly warm or at room temperature, with the labneh and extra dill and orange zest on top.

IRONY + BOE

PLEASE
WAIT HERE
UNTIL YOU
ARE USEFUL
—
THANK YOU

COURGETTE TORTILLA

A summery variation of the classic egg and potato tortilla, delicately
flavoured with mint, jamón and lemon zest.

Serves 6-8
4 small to medium courgettes, cut in half lengthways,
  deseeded and thinly sliced
8 tablespoons olive oil
1 garlic clove, thinly sliced
2 teaspoons shredded mint, plus extra to serve
100g jamón (page 281), finely chopped (optional)
6 organic or free-range eggs
finely grated zest of ½ lemon

Toss the courgette slices with ½ teaspoon of fine salt and leave in a colander
for 20 minutes to drain. Pat dry on kitchen paper. Heat 4 tablespoons of
the olive oil in a large, non-stick frying pan over a medium heat, add the
garlic and fry for 1 minute. Add the courgettes and continue to fry, stirring
occasionally, for about 10 minutes or until soft. Add the mint and the jamón,
if using, cook for 2 more minutes, then remove from the heat. Transfer the
mixture to a bowl, discarding any excess oil, and leave to cool.

Crack the eggs into a large bowl and lightly whisk with a tiny pinch
of salt and pepper. When the courgette mixture has cooled slightly, stir it
into the eggs. Wipe the frying pan clean and return to a medium to high heat.
When hot, add 2 more tablespoons of oil and swirl it around the pan and up
the sides to coat. Cook in exactly the same way as the Red Pepper Tortilla
(page 72), using the remaining 2 tablespoons of olive oil. When the tortilla
is ready, turn it out on to a clean plate. Serve slightly warm or at room
temperature, with extra mint and the lemon zest sprinkled on top.

PRAWN AND MUSHROOM REVUELTO

Revueltos are essentially scrambled eggs, present on many tapas boards throughout Spain. We use chanterelle and porcini mushrooms when in season from late summer to autumn. Any type of wild mushroom, or indeed oyster mushrooms, can be used for this recipe, as each adds a different quality.

Once you get the hang of making revueltos, you will find that many ingredients are interchangeable, so create your own combinations: prawns, jamón, chorizo, morcilla or salt cod with either asparagus, peas, spinach, mushrooms or artichokes. Because so much of the pleasure of the revueltos lies in the yielding texture, it is important that this is followed through with the added ingredients. The vegetables should be soft and melt in the mouth, while meats should be cut thinly.

Serves 4
3 tablespoons extra virgin olive oil
2 spring onions, finely chopped, including the green part
½ garlic clove, finely chopped
100g wild mushrooms or oyster mushrooms, sliced
4 organic or free-range eggs, plus 1 egg yolk
250g cooked North Atlantic prawns (page 281), shell-on, or about 125g peeled-weight
1 tablespoon roughly chopped flat-leaf parsley

Heat the oil in a large frying pan over a medium to high heat. Add the spring onions and garlic and sauté for a couple of minutes, until soft. Add the mushrooms and season with salt and pepper. Cook for a few minutes, stirring occasionally, until the mushrooms soften and release their juices. Cook for a further 5 minutes or until their liquid has reduced. Remove from the heat and stir in the eggs, egg yolk and prawns. Continue stirring off the heat until the mixture is creamy and pale and the egg is just cooked, returning the pan to the heat briefly if necessary. Check the seasoning, sprinkle with parsley and serve on toast or just as it is.

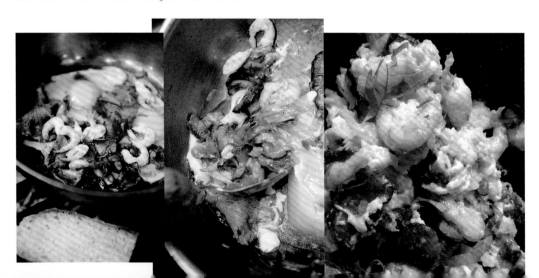

SEA URCHIN OR OYSTER REVUELTO

We get live sea urchins from the west coast of Ireland from November to February. They are delicate taste bombs of the sea, rivalled only by oysters, yet slightly sweeter. We use scissors to cut a hole in the underside before scooping out the miraculous roe and eating it raw or adding it to a revuelto.

Serves 4
3 tablespoons extra virgin olive oil
2 spring onions, finely chopped, including the green part
4 organic or free-range eggs
1 tablespoon sea urchin roe (page 281) or 4 shucked oysters, each sliced into 3
1 tablespoon finely shredded flat-leaf parsley

Heat the oil in a pan over a medium heat, add the spring onions and sauté for a couple of minutes, or until soft and sweet. Do not season the dish until the sea urchin roe has been added, as it tends to be quite salty and you may not need any extra salt. Reduce the heat to very low and stir in the eggs and the roe (or oysters). Continue stirring until the mixture looks creamy and pale and the egg is just cooked. Transfer to a plate, sprinkle over the chopped parsley and serve immediately. This dish is very creamy and rich due to the sea urchin roe, so we recommend you eat it with some toast.

SCAPE AND PRAWN REVUELTO

If you grow garlic, whether you are a farmer or an amateur, you will know that in summer the plants shoot up a flower stem, or scape. This needs cutting before the flower opens. It not only improves the quality of the garlic but the scapes taste great and have a wonderful texture too. In Spain scapes, known as *ajetes*, are mostly used in revueltos and can be bought in jars (page 281). In Turkey they are stewed slowly with lamb, potatoes and yoghurt.

Serves 4
170g fresh scapes (or use wild garlic leaves or spinach,
   prepared as for the Spinach and Jamón Tortilla on page 74)
4 organic or free-range eggs
300g cooked North Atlantic prawns (page 281), shell-on, or
   about 150g peeled-weight
1 tablespoon finely shredded flat-leaf parsley
3 tablespoons extra virgin olive oil

First prepare the scapes by removing the flower heads, if they have not already been removed. The base of the stem is thicker and can be fibrous, so, in a similar technique to trimming asparagus, snap off the end where it becomes easy to do so. Discard these tough ends and cut the rest into 2cm pieces. Place in a small saucepan, just cover with water and simmer with the lid on for 15 minutes. Drain the scapes, reserving one tablespoon of the cooking water, and season with salt and pepper.

Crack the eggs into a bowl, add the prawns and parsley and beat briefly with a wooden spoon to break up the eggs a little and mix everything through. Place a medium non-stick pan over a medium heat and add the olive oil and the scapes. Fry for 30 seconds, then pour in the egg mix. Give it a brief stir, count to 15, give another brief stir and continue in this way until the eggs are just cooked. Serve immediately.

ANCHOVY, EGG AND HARISSA BRIK

North African warka dough is a little fiddly to make but worth it for the delicacy of the pastry. You can use single filo sheets instead if practice and time are limited.

Makes 2 briks / serves 2-4

WARKA DOUGH

300g organic strong white bread flour (Shipton Mill or Doves Farm)

1 tablespoon olive oil

2 teaspoons white wine vinegar

250ml tepid water

FILLING

4 tablespoons olive oil

2 teaspoons Harissa (page 176), plus extra to serve

2 handfuls of coriander leaves, plus extra to serve

2-4 best-quality (Ortiz) salted anchovy fillets (page 281)

2 organic or free-range eggs

First make the warka dough. Sift the flour into a large bowl. Mix the oil, vinegar and water in a jug and gradually add it to the flour in small quantities, working the dough with your fingertips to remove any lumps that form. By the time all the liquid has been added, you should have a loose, wet but smooth dough. Now begin to work the dough with your hand cupped in a claw shape. Knead like this for 3-4 minutes, until you have a wet, sticky and elastic dough. Cover and place in the fridge to rest for 20-30 minutes.

To make the warka sheets, you will need a saucepan and a non-stick frying pan that fits snugly over the top. Fill the saucepan halfway with water and bring to the boil. Place the frying pan on top of the saucepan and heat for a few minutes. (Make sure the water is not touching the frying pan.)

Take the dough out of the fridge and knead it for 10-15 seconds. Tear off a piece about the size of a lemon and hold it with one hand. This sounds easier than it is; the dough is very moist and you will feel it slipping away from your hand, so try to find a way of holding it without dropping it.

Imagine you are using the dough like a paintbrush and dab it on to the hot pan, lifting it up after a couple of seconds to leave a residue and dabbing it immediately on to an adjacent area to form another small circle. Repeat the process until the base of the pan is covered, creating a circle roughly 20cm in diameter with no gaps. Try not to dab the dough twice in the same area as it can tear and lift. Now prise off the edges of this circle with your nails, peel it off and place on a plate lined with a piece of baking parchment. Repeat the process one more time, separating the 2 warka sheets with another piece of baking parchment. If you have any remaining dough, place it in a container and return it to the fridge. It will keep for 2-3 days. If you are not using your warka sheets immediately, place on a plate and wrap in cling film.

To make the brik, heat half the olive oil in a shallow, preferably non-stick, frying pan over a low to medium heat. Place 1 warka sheet in the pan and put a line of half the harissa, half the coriander leaves and half the anchovy fillets across the middle of it, just off centre. Now crack an egg more or less on top of the anchovy, again just off centre, and fold over the empty half of the warka to form a half-moon shape. Seal the edges with your fingers. Fry the brik for a couple of minutes, until golden brown underneath, then turn over and repeat on the other side. Remove the brik from the pan using a spatula and place on kitchen paper to absorb any excess oil. Repeat to cook the other brik. Serve immediately, with more harissa and coriander.

Dairy

HOMEMADE LABNEH

Labneh is strained yoghurt, popular in the Eastern Mediterranean, that
is eaten as a dip or dried further and eaten like a cheese. Unspiced and
unsalted, it is delicious at breakfast with honey. Labneh differs from region
to region. This version is light and fresh, similar to cream cheese in
texture but still with the acidity of yoghurt. We have recently experimented
with leaving it above our charcoal grill to develop a subtle smoky flavour.
We think labneh is a must in some guise on a mezze table.

SPICED LABNEH

This spiced version is a Lebanese recipe.

Serves 4
500g strained Greek yoghurt, such as Total
½ teaspoon fine sea salt
1 green chilli, deseeded and finely chopped
1½ teaspoons fenugreek seeds, boiled for 30 minutes in 3
   changes of water to get rid of their bitterness
2 teaspoons black onion seeds

Place the yoghurt in a bowl, add the salt and mix well. Line a separate bowl
with a fine (muslin) cloth large enough to hang over the sides. Spoon the
yoghurt into the centre of the lined bowl, bring the corners of the cloth
together and secure tightly with string or a strong elastic band. Suspend the
muslin-wrapped yoghurt over the bowl and leave for 6 hours if using yoghurt
that is already strained or longer if the yoghurt is thinner.

Unwrap the labneh and scrape into a bowl. Mix in the chilli, fenugreek
and black onion seeds. To serve, spread the labneh on a plate, drizzle
with some extra virgin olive oil and accompany with bread and any of the
following:

- lots of fresh raw vegetables and sweet herbs
- Roast Beetroot (page 98)
- Fried aubergines with chilli and mint (page 146)
- broad beans, rocket and mint dressed with lemon and olive oil
- pickled baby aubergines stuffed with walnuts, chilli and mint

TETILLA CHEESE WITH FIG AND WALNUT JAM

Tetilla cheese is a constant at Morito. Traditionally made in Galicia, its
name translates as 'teat', so called because of its cone-like shape. It is
made from pasteurised cow's milk and is smooth and creamy on the palate. To
griddle tetilla at home, all you need is a searing-hot pan so the cheese will
quickly develop a crust and yet will not melt away. The point of this dish is
the wonderful textural transformation that happens when the cheese is seared,
as well as the way the sweet acids of the fruit cut through the richness.
Membrillo (quince cheese) or runny honey is also delicious with tetilla when
fresh figs are not in season.

Serves 4
4 slices of tetilla cheese (page 281), about 1.5cm thick

FIG AND WALNUT JAM (or 30g membrillo, page 281)
6 fresh black figs (about 300g), peeled and roughly chopped
100g caster sugar
juice and zest of 1 lemon
1 cinnamon stick
10 walnut halves, slightly crushed

To make the jam, place the figs, sugar, lemon juice, zest and cinnamon stick
in a pan and cook gently over a low heat for around 5 minutes. When the figs
release their juices, increase the heat to medium and continue to cook until
the jam thickens a little. Stir the mixture regularly to prevent it sticking.
After around 10 minutes, it should have a jam-like consistency but be fresher
and crunchier. Remove from the heat and stir in the walnuts.

Place a large griddle pan or frying pan over a medium to high heat.
When the pan is very hot, add the slices of tetilla and allow them to develop
a golden crust underneath (in our experience it is better to cook the cheese
straight from the fridge). Using a spatula, turn the cheese, then cook until
the other side is coloured. Gently remove the cheese and serve immediately,
while hot and soft in the middle, with the jam or membrillo on the side.

HALLOUMI, GRILLED ONION AND OLIVE SALAD

Cook the halloumi at the last minute to preserve that perfect textural
balance of melted cheese that is still soft, chewy and slightly squeaky.
The pungent saltiness of the halloumi goes beautifully with the sweet onion.

Serves 4
1 quantity of Grilled Onion Salad dressed with Pomegranate
   Dressing (page 123) or lemon juice and olive oil dressing
1 tablespoon chopped lemon thyme or ordinary thyme
225-250g block of halloumi, sliced lengthways into 8 pieces
a handful of black olives
a handful of mint, shredded

First prepare the onion salad. When you are ready to eat, rub the thyme all
over the slices of halloumi. Place a griddle pan or large frying pan over a
high heat (or you can use a barbecue). When hot, lay the slices of halloumi
in the pan (or on the barbecue) and cook for 2-3 minutes on either side until
seared but soft in the middle. Remove and serve immediately with the grilled
onion salad, black olives and mint.

VEGETABLES

BEETROOT BORANI

Borani, the Iranian yoghurt dip, is an opulent dish for the senses:
delectable, visually stunning and guaranteed to win over the hearts of
beetroot sceptics. A firm favourite on the Morito menu.

Serves 4
4 medium raw bunched beetroot (about 700g)
1 small garlic clove, crushed to a paste with ½ teaspoon salt
4 tablespoons extra virgin olive oil, plus extra for
  drizzling
4 tablespoons strained Greek yoghurt, such as Total
2 tablespoons chopped dill, plus a few sprigs to garnish
2 tablespoons Forum Cabernet Sauvignon vinegar (page 280), or
  a good-quality aged red wine vinegar with a pinch of sugar
50g feta cheese, crumbled
6 walnut halves, roughly crushed
½ teaspoon black onion seeds

Wash the beetroot but don't peel it, then put in a pan, cover with water and
bring to the boil. Cook for about 40 minutes or until tender, topping up the
water if necessary. The beetroot is ready when a sharp knife goes through
easily. Drain and leave to cool. Peel the beetroot and blend in a food
processor. You want some texture in the purée, so don't over-blend. Transfer
to a bowl, add the garlic, olive oil, yoghurt, dill, vinegar and a pinch
of salt and mix well. Check the seasoning and spread the purée on a plate.
Sprinkle with the feta, walnuts, black onion seeds and extra sprigs of dill
and drizzle with a little olive oil. Serve with Flatbread (page 10) or pitta.

BEETROOT, ALMONDS AND MINT

At Morito we often serve this salad with a few thin slices of cecina (Spanish cured beef, page 281) or Pastirma (pages 230-1). However, it's so delicious on its own that it is difficult to stop eating.

Serves 4
3 tablespoons blanched almonds or roasted Marcona (page 281)
700g raw bunched beetroot, peeled and coarsely grated
1 quantity of Pomegranate Dressing (page 123)
2 tablespoons shredded mint
2 tablespoons fresh pomegranate seeds

If using blanched almonds, roast them in the oven at 150°C/300°F/Gas 2 until golden brown. Cool and roughly chop.

Place the grated beetroot in a bowl. Pour the dressing over, then add the almonds, mint and pomegranate seeds. Mix well, taste and serve.

ROAST BEETROOT AND GREEN MAYONNAISE

Roast beetroot is also delicious with Spiced Labneh (page 91).

> **Serves 4**
> 800g raw bunched beetroot, peeled and cut into small wedges
> 3 tablespoons olive oil
> 1 tablespoon Forum Cabernet Sauvignon vinegar (page 280), or
>   a good-quality aged red wine vinegar with a pinch of sugar
> 1 quantity of Green Mayonnaise (below)

Preheat the oven to 200°C/400°F/Gas 6. Place the beetroot in a baking tray, toss with the olive oil, season with salt and pepper and put into the hot oven. Cook for 1-1½ hours, until soft and slightly shrivelled. You want the beetroot to develop a chewy texture and a concentrated sweet flavour. If you think it might start to burn, cover with foil for a while and then take it off when the beetroot is nearly done.

Toss the beetroot with the vinegar and serve warm or at room temperature, with the green mayonnaise on the side.

GREEN MAYONNAISE

> **Serves 4**
> 1 bunch of basil, roughly chopped
> 1 bunch of tarragon, roughly chopped
> 1 bunch of dill, roughly chopped
> 4 tablespoons extra virgin olive oil
> 1 tablespoon Moscatel vinegar (page 280),
>   or another aged sweet wine vinegar
> a pinch of sugar
> 3 tablespoons Alioli (page 161), made
>   without the garlic, or mayonnaise

Blitz all the ingredients except the alioli in a blender until smooth. Transfer to a bowl and mix in the alioli or mayonnaise. Check for seasoning.

SPINACH AND LEMON SALAD

We love this salad, but we acknowledge that it is intense, highly zesty and not for everybody. The quick brining the lemon receives has a softening effect on both the texture and the taste. Excellent alongside fried fish, prawns or Lamb Chops Mechoui or Fried Chickpeas (pages 220 and 108).

Serves 4
2 tablespoons sugar
500ml water
½ lemon, cut into quarters
4 tablespoons extra virgin olive oil
500g spinach or chard, washed and drained, leaves only
1 tablespoon lemon juice

To make a brine, dissolve the sugar and 2 tablespoons of salt in the water, mixing with your fingertips. With a sharp knife, lightly trim the thin core of each lemon segment, as this can be a bit tough and it then makes it easier to remove any pips. Slice each wedge across into thin triangles. Stir them into the brine and leave to soften for 40 minutes to 1 hour. Drain well.

Place a large pot over a high heat and add 1 tablespoon of the olive oil. When it is hot, add the spinach or chard and a small pinch of salt. Stir until the spinach has collapsed and is just tender. Drain in a colander if necessary and then spread the spinach over a baking tray or large plate to cool. When cool, squeeze out any excess water.

Dress the spinach with the remaining olive oil, lemon juice and salt to taste. Serve with the softened lemon on top.

SPINACH, PINE NUTS, RAISINS AND ANCHOVIES

A classic tapa from Seville.

Serves 4

BREADCRUMBS

- 500ml olive or sunflower oil, for deep-frying
- 1 pitta bread, sliced into thin strips
- 1 garlic clove, finely chopped

SPINACH

- 400g spinach or chard
- 4 tablespoons olive oil
- 1 garlic clove, finely chopped
- 2 sprigs of thyme, finely chopped
- 1 sprig of rosemary, finely chopped
- 2 bay leaves, preferably fresh
- 2 medium red onions, thinly sliced
- 2 tablespoons Forum Cabernet Sauvignon vinegar (page 280), or a good-quality aged red wine vinegar with a pinch of sugar
- 3-4 best-quality (Ortiz) salted anchovy fillets, finely chopped (page 281)
- 1 tablespoon pine nuts, lightly toasted
- 1 tablespoon raisins, soaked in warm water till plump, drained

To make the breadcrumbs, heat the oil in a large saucepan and add the sliced pitta bread. Fry over a medium heat until golden. Remove from the pan and place on kitchen paper to absorb any excess oil. Add the chopped garlic to the pan and fry for a few seconds until just golden. Do not let the garlic get too dark or it will taste bitter. Remove from the oil with a slotted spoon and place on kitchen paper (the oil can be kept to use again). Using a pestle and mortar or food processor, crush the pitta bread with the garlic into large crumbs. Set aside.

Fill a large saucepan with water and bring to a rolling boil with 1 teaspoon of salt. Add the spinach or chard and blanch for a minute. Remove with a slotted spoon and drain in a colander. When cool enough to handle, squeeze gently to get rid of any excess water.

Heat the olive oil in a pan and add the garlic, thyme, rosemary and bay leaves, followed by the red onions and a pinch of salt. Cook for 10-15 minutes over a medium-high heat, stirring occasionally. When the onions have softened and become sweet, add the vinegar and cook for 1 minute. Stir in the anchovies, followed by the pine nuts, raisins, spinach and a pinch of black pepper. Heat up and stir well. Sprinkle the breadcrumbs on top and serve.

SPINACH, FENNEL AND HERB PIE

We had never come across this pastry before. It is a Cretan speciality from our wonderful chef, Marianna. Simple to make and rich and crumbly in the mouth, it is an excellent addition to our modest pastry repertoire.

Serves 8

FILLING

5 tablespoons olive oil
2 fennel bulbs, finely diced
2 red onions, finely diced
1 bunch of spring onions, finely chopped
1 leek, finely chopped
1 teaspoon fennel seeds, roughly ground
400g spinach, finely chopped
2 bunches of dill, chopped
1 bunch of mint, chopped
2 organic or free-range eggs, beaten
80g feta, crumbled

PASTRY

500g plain flour, sifted, plus extra for dusting
200ml olive oil
200ml warm water
1 organic or free-range egg, beaten
2 tablespoons sesame seeds

Heat the olive oil for the filling in a large saucepan over a medium heat and add the fennel, red onions, spring onions, leek, fennel seeds and ½ teaspoon of salt. Cook over a low-medium heat for 20-30 minutes, stirring often, until soft and sweet. In a bowl, mix the spinach, dill and mint with a pinch of salt. When the onion and fennel mix is ready, remove from the heat and mix in the spinach and herbs. Leave to cool, then stir in the egg and the feta. Check the seasoning and set aside.

To make the pastry, place the flour and 1 level teaspoon of salt in a large bowl. Mix the olive oil and water together and gradually add it to the flour. Mix until a soft dough is achieved, but do not over-work it or the pastry will be heavy. Cover the dough with a cloth and let it rest for 20 minutes.

Preheat the oven to 180°C/350°F/Gas 4. Turn out the dough on to a work surface dusted with flour and separate it into 2 balls, making one slightly larger than the other. Roll out the larger ball of dough to about 5mm thick. Oil a 25-30cm pie dish and press the pastry into the dish, letting it hang over the sides, and spread the filling evenly. Now roll out the remaining dough also 5mm thick. Place on top of the filling and fuse the pastry edges together with your thumb and trim off the extra. Brush the pie with the beaten egg, sprinkle with the sesame seeds and make a couple of holes in the top to let out the steam. Place in the oven for about 1 hour, until golden brown and crisp. Serve hot or cold.

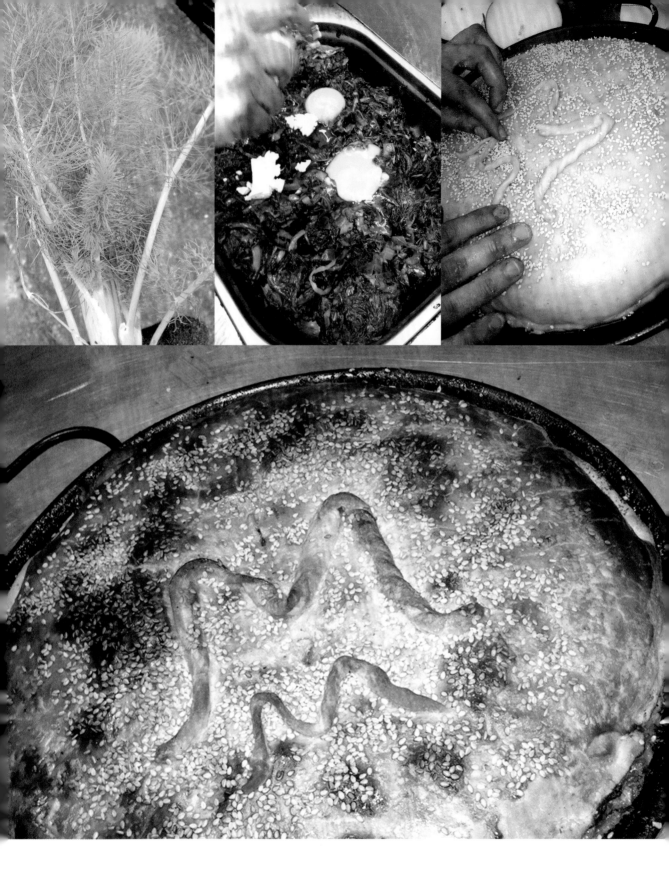

CAULIFLOWER, TOMATO AND CUMIN

In our opinion British cauliflower is the best in the world and we are sure that beings from Mars would think it the most exotic and extraordinary-looking vegetable on this planet, yet most of us don't even give it a second thought. Cauliflower is special because one can eat it raw for amazing crunch and subtle peppery taste, barely cooked and deliciously dressed, as in this recipe, or slow-cooked as in the next.

Serves 4
250g sweet cherry tomatoes
1 small cauliflower, leaves and stalk discarded, separated
   into small florets
1 small bunch of coriander, leaves picked

TOMATO DRESSING
200g sweet cherry tomatoes
4 tablespoons extra virgin olive oil
½ tablespoon sweet red wine vinegar like Forum or Moscatel
   vinegar (page 280), or lemon juice
2 teaspoons cumin seeds, lightly toasted and ground (page 34)
a pinch of sugar

Bring a large pan of water to a rolling boil. Blanch the tomatoes in it for 10 seconds, then remove with a slotted spoon and place under cold running water to cool. Peel off the skins, cut the tomatoes in quarters, then roughly scoop out the seeds and discard. Now blanch the cauliflower in the same water. Place the florets in the pot with ½ teaspoon of salt and simmer for a couple of minutes, until just cooked. Drain in a colander and cool.

To make the dressing, place the tomatoes in a food processor (or use a hand-held blender) and blitz until completely smooth. Transfer to a jam jar with a lid, add the olive oil, vinegar or lemon juice, cumin, sugar and a pinch of salt and shake well.

Just before serving, transfer the cauliflower to a bowl, add the tomatoes and pour over the dressing. Sprinkle with the coriander, mix everything together and check the seasoning.

CAULIFLOWER, PINE NUTS, RAISINS AND SAFFRON

The cauliflower becomes soft and rich from absorbing the flavoursome oil.

Serves 4
4 tablespoons olive oil
1 Spanish onion, sliced
1 small cauliflower, leaves and stalk discarded, separated
   into florets
1 garlic clove, thinly sliced
a large pinch of ground turmeric
½ teaspoon cumin seeds, lightly toasted and roughly ground
   (page 34)
½ teaspoon coriander seeds, roughly ground
4 tablespoons pine nuts
3 tablespoons raisins, soaked in hot water till plump, drained
15 threads of saffron, steeped in 100ml hot water
1 small bunch of coriander, roughly chopped

Heat the oil in a large, wide saucepan over a medium heat, add the onion and
a pinch of salt and cook for about 15 minutes, stirring frequently, until
soft, golden and sweet. Add the cauliflower florets, garlic, spices and another
pinch of salt. Cook over a medium heat for 10-15 minutes, stirring often.

   Now add the pine nuts, raisins and the saffron-infused water. Cover the
pan and cook, stirring occasionally, for a further 10 minutes or until the
cauliflower is tender. Stir in half of the chopped coriander and remove from
the heat. Serve with the remaining coriander scattered on top.

RHUBARB AND TARRAGON SALAD

In Istanbul, in May, street vendors sell a spiky type of wild rhubarb. Passers-by buy it for a snack. First the knobbly skin is peeled off and then the rhubarb is dipped in salt and eaten to accompany a rich lamb kebab or fish. If you use young, tender rhubarb you will not have to peel it. Slice some thinly to check and see what you think.

Serves 4
300g young, thinnish rhubarb stalks
1 small bunch of tarragon, leaves picked
a small squeeze of lemon (about 2 teaspoons)
2 tablespoons extra virgin olive oil

Give the rhubarb a wash, then top and tail it. Slice thinly and toss it in a bowl with the tarragon. When you're ready to eat, season with salt and pepper, then mix in the lemon juice and olive oil.

HUMMUS

Noelia helped us with our food stall outside Morito for a long time. She used to make the hummus almost every day with incredible, brutal efficiency. It was by far the most delicious hummus we have ever tasted. This is her version. At the restaurant we pressure-cook soaked chickpeas with half an onion and some salt, similar to how tinned chickpeas are made, so in this recipe we recommend using tinned chickpeas.

Serves 4
juice of 1 lemon
400g tin of cooked chickpeas, drained and rinsed
1 large garlic clove, crushed to a paste with 1 teaspoon salt
5 tablespoons extra virgin olive oil
1½ tablespoons tahini

Put all the ingredients into a deep, narrow bowl or jug with a little splash of water and, using a hand-held blender, purée until smooth. If you do not have a hand-held blender, use a liquidiser. Check the seasoning and serve with crudités or Spiced Lamb (page 218), Chopped Salad (page 108) and toasted pine nuts (page 35).

FRIED CHICKPEAS AND CHOPPED SALAD

The gorgeous chef David Cook first enlightened us about the joys of fried chickpeas. Rather annoyingly, though, only chickpeas in jars produce the really delicious finished article. We don't know why. This dish very quickly became a Morito summer classic.

Serves 4-6

FRIED CHICKPEAS

500ml olive, sunflower or rapeseed oil for frying

425g jarred chickpeas (page 281), (drained weight), rinsed

¼ teaspoon freshly ground cinnamon

¼ teaspoon freshly ground coriander seeds

¼ teaspoon freshly ground cumin seeds

CHOPPED SALAD

1 small cucumber, half peeled in strips, deseeded and diced small

½ red onion, finely chopped

250g cherry tomatoes, quartered

½ bunch of coriander, shredded

2 red or green chillies, deseeded and finely chopped

4 tablespoons extra virgin olive oil

juice of 1 lemon

To cook the chickpeas, heat the oil in a large saucepan, making sure it comes no more than halfway up the side. Dry the chickpeas on kitchen paper to prevent the oil spitting when you add them. When the oil is hot but not smoking – around 180°C/350°F or when a test chickpea sizzles furiously in it – add the chickpeas and fry until they are puffed up, golden brown and crisp. Remove from the oil with a slotted spoon and place in a bowl lined with kitchen paper to absorb any excess oil. Sprinkle the spices over the chickpeas, season with salt and toss well. Keep hot.

Quickly dress the chopped salad: put the vegetables, coriander and chillies in a bowl, add the olive oil and lemon juice and stir well. Season to taste. Transfer the chopped salad to a dish, spoon the hot chickpeas over the top and serve immediately.

FRIED CHICKPEAS, BUTTERNUT SQUASH AND TAHINI

And an autumnal version.

Serves 4
1 butternut squash (about 800g), peeled, deseeded and cut
    into 1cm cubes
2 tablespoons olive oil
½ teaspoon ground cinnamon
1 quantity of Fried Chickpeas (see previous recipe, but fry
    the chickpeas to order)
½ red onion, thinly sliced
½ bunch of coriander, finely shredded
1 quantity of Tahini Yoghurt (page 244)
½ teaspoon black onion seeds

Preheat the oven to 200°C/400°F/Gas 6. Place the squash in a bowl, toss with
the oil, cinnamon and some salt and pepper and transfer to a baking tray.
Roast for 20-30 minutes, until the squash is soft and the edges are slightly
crisp. Keep warm.

   A couple of minutes before serving, fry the chickpeas as in the previous
recipe, seasoning with the spices. Mix the hot chickpeas with the squash,
red onion and half the coriander, then check the seasoning. Pour the tahini
yoghurt all over and sprinkle the remaining coriander and black onion seeds
on top.

FALAFEL

Nothing has quite surpassed our favourite falafel experience on the back streets of Cairo. Our friends Ali and Rebecca made it their mission to show us the best. The Egyptian name for falafel is *taameya*, and the stall we remember most was run by a proud Amazonian woman. We stood there for hours watching her technique and noting down the ingredients. We serve our falafel with green tahini and pickles.

Makes 12-16 falafel / serves 4
200g dried shelled fava beans (page 281), or dried chickpeas,
**   soaked in cold water for a minimum of 6 hours, or overnight**
1 medium leek, green part only, chopped
1 medium bunch of dill, roughly chopped
1 medium bunch of coriander, leaves only
1 medium bunch of flat-leaf parsley, roughly chopped
2 garlic cloves, crushed to a paste with 1 teaspoon salt
2 small spring onions, including the green part, chopped
2 teaspoons coriander seeds, roughly ground
1½ teaspoons cumin seeds, roughly ground
1 teaspoon baking powder
2 tablespoons sesame seeds
1 litre sunflower, rapeseed or olive oil for deep-frying

Drain the fava beans or chickpeas and transfer to a food processor along with all the other ingredients except the spices, baking powder, sesame seeds and oil. Add 1½ teaspoons of salt and blitz until bright green and almost smooth. The mixture should be moist and thick, like cream cheese but a little coarser. Transfer to a bowl, stir in the spices and baking powder, and check the seasoning. Now take a bit of the mixture the size of a small walnut and shape into a flattish disc. Sprinkle with sesame seeds and set aside. Repeat with the remaining mixture.

To fry the falafel, fill a deep-fat fryer or large saucepan to halfway with the oil and heat until hot but not smoking; it should be about 180°C/350°F. Lower in half the falafel using a slotted spoon, and fry for a few minutes, until golden brown and crisp on the outside, soft and cooked in the middle. It is important not to have the oil too hot, otherwise the falafel will be dark and crisp on the outside but still raw in the middle. Transfer to kitchen paper to drain. Repeat with the remaining falafel. Serve immediately with the Green Tahini (opposite), Turkish pickled chillies (page 280) or Homemade Pickles (page 30) and, if you wish, Chopped Salad (page 108).

GREEN TAHINI

Serves 4

1 small bunch of dill, roughly chopped

1 small bunch of tarragon, roughly chopped

1 small bunch of basil, roughly chopped

1 small bunch of flat-leaf parsley, roughly chopped

1 garlic clove, crushed to a paste with ½ teaspoon salt

6 tablespoons extra virgin olive oil

200g strained Greek yoghurt, such as Total

2 tablespoons pale tahini

juice of ½ lemon

1 tablespoon Moscatel vinegar (page 280) or good-quality
   white wine vinegar

a good pinch of sugar

Place the herbs, garlic and olive oil in a food processor or use a hand-held
blender and blitz to a smooth green paste. Transfer to a bowl and add all
the remaining ingredients. Mix well, season with a little salt and check the
seasoning. The ideal consistency is that of double cream. If the sauce is too
thick, add a splash of water.

TURKISH CHOPPED SALAD, YOGHURT
AND CHILLI BUTTER

Chopped salad is a classic recipe from Mangal, our favourite Ocakbasi Turkish restaurant in Dalston. It is fantastic with Lamb Chops Mechoui (page 220). We have recently added a few chopped pickles to the salad to give it extra zing.

Serves 4

CHOPPED SALAD

½ cucumber, half peeled in strips, deseeded and finely diced

6 radishes, halved and thinly sliced

1 small red onion, finely diced

250g cherry tomatoes, cut into sixths

50g pickled beetroot, chopped (optional)

1 red chilli, cut in half lengthways, deseeded and finely chopped

3 Turkish pickled chillies (page 280), thinly sliced (optional)

1 bunch of flat-leaf parsley, finely shredded

1 bunch of mint, finely shredded

100g purslane (page 281), roughly chopped (optional)

100g rocket, roughly chopped

100ml extra virgin olive oil

juice of 1 lemon

200g strained Greek yoghurt, such as Total

1 small garlic clove, crushed to a paste with ½ teaspoon salt

CHILLI BUTTER

60g butter

1 teaspoon Aleppo chilli flakes (page 280) or cayenne pepper

For the chilli butter, melt the butter in a small saucepan over a medium heat. When the whey evaporates and the butter turns golden brown, it has caramelised. Remove and stir in the chilli flakes or cayenne. Keep warm.

Just before serving, place all the vegetables, herbs and salad leaves in a bowl, add the oil and lemon juice, season with salt and pepper and toss well. Mix the yoghurt with the crushed garlic and loosen with a splash of water if it is too thick. Pour the yoghurt over the salad, then spoon the warm chilli butter on the yoghurt.

THE FOUR SEASONS OF TABBOULEH

The classic tabbouleh is a summery salad, but there are also seasonal
variations for spring, autumn and winter.

Serves 4

SPRING

70g bulgur
150g fresh peas, podded and blanched briefly
150g fresh small broad beans, podded and blanched (page 130)
5 asparagus spears, cut into 1cm pieces and blanched briefly
4 sour plums (page 27), diced (optional)
3 spring onions, sliced into thin rounds
1 bunch of flat-leaf parsley, finely shredded
1 bunch of mint, finely shredded
1 bunch of dill, roughly chopped

DRESSING

½ garlic clove, crushed to a paste with a little salt
¼ teaspoon ground cinnamon
2 tablespoons lemon juice
4 tablespoons extra virgin olive oil

SUMMER

70g bulgur
350g sweet cherry tomatoes, diced
¼ cucumber, peeled, deseeded and diced small
3 spring onions, sliced into thin rounds
1 bunch of flat-leaf parsley, finely shredded
1 bunch of mint, finely shredded

DRESSING

½ garlic clove, crushed to a paste with a little salt
¼ teaspoon ground cinnamon
2 tablespoons lemon juice
4 tablespoons extra virgin olive oil

AUTUMN

70g bulgur

250g white muscat or sultana grapes, halved and deseeded

3 fresh figs, peeled and diced

150g almonds or walnuts, lightly roasted and roughly chopped

4 spring onions, sliced into thin rounds

1 bunch of flat-leaf parsley, finely shredded

1 bunch of mint, finely shredded

DRESSING

½ garlic clove, crushed to a paste with a little salt

¼ teaspoon ground cinnamon

½ tablespoon lemon juice

2 tablespoons verjus (page 280)

4 tablespoons extra virgin olive oil

WINTER

70g bulgur

seeds of 1 large pomegranate

150g walnuts, roughly chopped

4 tablespoons shredded red chicory or radicchio

½ small cauliflower, cut into tiny florets

1 small fennel bulb, finely chopped

4 spring onions, sliced into thin rounds

1 bunch of flat-leaf parsley, finely shredded

1 bunch of mint, finely shredded

DRESSING

1 quantity of Pomegranate Dressing (page 123)

½ garlic clove, crushed to a paste with a little salt

¼ teaspoon ground cinnamon

TO ASSEMBLE THE TABBOULEH

Put the bulgur in a bowl, add enough cold water just to cover and let it sit for 10 minutes. Meanwhile, put all the dressing ingredients in a jar with a lid, season with salt and pepper and shake well. When the bulgur has absorbed the water and is soft, gently rub it between the palms of your hands to fluff it up. Place the remaining salad ingredients in a large bowl and pour over the dressing. Add the bulgur to the salad and mix well. Check the seasoning and serve.

one Like j
uts very fac
out taking t

ated Equa
s Are Mor
hers"

Animal Fo

FATTOUSH

Fattoush is one of the great salads of the world. It sings of the summer, with crunchy, fresh, sweet vegetables and herbs. Our version has been tweaked and refined over the years.

Serves 4

FATTOUSH

25g butter, melted

1 large Middle Eastern flatbread (about 20cm in diameter),
  or 1–2 pitta breads, split in half lengthways

½ cucumber, half peeled in strips, deseeded and diced small

½ small cauliflower, cut into tiny florets

10 sweet cherry tomatoes, cut into quarters or sixths

6 red radishes, cut into quarters or sixths

1 spring onion, sliced into thin rounds

100g purslane (page 281), available in Turkish/Middle Eastern
  shops in the summer, whole leaves only (optional)

1 bunch of flat-leaf parsley, shredded

1 bunch of mint, shredded

1 bunch of coriander, shredded

½ teaspoon za'atar (page 280)

DRESSING

6 tablespoons extra virgin olive oil

1 tablespoon pomegranate molasses (page 280)

1 tablespoon Forum Cabernet Sauvignon vinegar (page 280),
  or a good-quality aged red wine vinegar with a pinch of
  sugar

2 tablespoons freshly squeezed pomegranate
  juice (opposite)

1 teaspoon sumac (page 280)

1 teaspoon za'atar (page 280)

a pinch of ground cinnamon

a pinch of sugar

Preheat the oven to 180°C/350°F/Gas 4. Brush the melted butter on both sides of the flatbreads or pittas. Bake them in the oven for 10-15 minutes, until golden and crisp. Remove from the oven and set aside to cool.

To make the dressing, put all the ingredients in a jam jar with a lid and shake well. Taste for seasoning. Put the vegetables and herbs in a bowl and pour over the dressing. Lightly crush the crisp flatbread into the bowl, mix well and serve immediately, sprinkled with the ½ teaspoon of za'atar.

RADISH AND POMEGRANATE SALAD

This pretty, peppery salad gives sweetness to your table and is excellent alongside fish, chicken or a rich vegetable dish. We slice the vegetables on a mandoline, as the thinner they are, the better they absorb the dressing.

Serves 4

POMEGRANATE DRESSING

freshly squeezed juice of 1 large pomegranate

1 tablespoon Forum Cabernet Sauvignon vinegar (page 280), or a good-quality aged red wine vinegar with a pinch of sugar

2 tablespoons pomegranate molasses (page 280)

4 tablespoons extra virgin olive oil

SALAD

150–200g long white daikon (mooli) or black radish (page 281), thinly sliced

5 red radishes, sliced into very thin rounds

1 golden beetroot, peeled and very thinly sliced (optional)

1 small kohlrabi, peeled, cut in half and thinly sliced

1 bunch of mint, finely shredded

3 tablespoons pomegranate seeds

To make the fresh pomegranate juice, cut the pomegranate in half and take out the seeds, discarding any bitter skin or white pith. Put the seeds in a sieve and press them with the back of spoon to extract all the juice, discarding any skin or hard seeds. Put all the dressing ingredients into a jam jar with a lid, season with salt and pepper and shake well.

To make the salad, put the radishes, beetroot, if using, and kohlrabi in a bowl, add the mint and pomegranate seeds and pour over the dressing. Mix everything together and serve immediately.

SETAS ALIÑADAS (MARINATED MUSHROOMS)

Oyster mushrooms have quite a dry texture, so when you sear them in a pan they colour pleasingly without releasing any juices. This caramelisation transforms the flavour of what is a fairly ordinary mushroom into something special. The mushrooms are then dressed – *aliñadas* – with the olive oil, vinegar, garlic, onions and herbs.

Serves 4

500g oyster mushrooms or a mix of oyster and wild mushrooms, if available, cleaned and any thick stalks trimmed

4 tablespoons extra virgin olive oil

2 teaspoons Forum Cabernet Sauvignon vinegar (page 280), or a good-quality aged red wine vinegar with a pinch of sugar

1 garlic clove, very finely chopped

¼ red onion, very finely chopped

a handful of flat-leaf parsley, finely shredded

1 teaspoon dried oregano

100g jamón ibérico (pages 49 and 281), cut into thin strips (optional)

Place the mushrooms in a bowl and toss with salt, pepper and half of the olive oil. Heat a wide frying pan over a high heat. When the pan is extremely hot, add half the mushrooms in a single layer, gill side down, and press down with a spatula or spoon. When they are browned on one side and just cooked, transfer to a bowl and repeat with the remaining mushrooms, remembering not to overcrowd them in the pan. Toss the cooked mushrooms with the remaining oil, the vinegar, garlic, onion and herbs. Season once more, if necessary, and serve with the jamón strips on top, if using.

GRILLED COURGETTE SALAD, SUMAC AND PINE NUTS

We like to use the pale (white) courgettes or a mixture of yellow, green and white during the summer when we have a choice.

> **Serves 4**
> **4 large courgettes**
> **4 tablespoons extra virgin olive oil**
> **juice of ½ lemon**
> **½ teaspoon sumac (page 280), plus extra for sprinkling**
> **2 tablespoons pine nuts, lightly toasted (page 35)**
> **1 bunch of mint, finely shredded**

Cut the courgettes in quarters lengthways and scoop out the seeds. Place in a colander, toss with ½ teaspoon of salt and leave for 20 minutes.

Preheat the grill to its highest setting, prepare a medium to hot barbecue, or place a griddle pan over a high heat. Grill the courgettes until just soft and slightly charred underneath, then turn over and grill the other side. Remove from the heat, place on a chopping board and slice at an angle into smaller strips. Place the courgettes in a bowl, add the olive oil, lemon juice, sumac, pine nuts, mint and a little more salt if needed. Toss everything together and serve with extra sumac sprinkled over.

GRILLED ONION SALAD, POMEGRANATES AND MINT

If we are proud of anything in our books, it is making people think about vegetables in different ways and all their possibilities. This recipe is a good example of that. Charred onions have a beautifully smoky taste and a wonderful velvety texture. Please do try this dish.

Serves 4
4-6 medium red or white onions
1 quantity of Pomegranate Dressing (page 123)
seeds of 1 large pomegranate
2 tablespoons shredded mint

Grill the onions whole and unpeeled over a hot barbecue for 20-30 minutes, until black and charred all over. This method will impart an aromatic smokiness to the dish. Cool slightly, peel and cut into halves or quarters.

Alternatively, if roasting in the oven, preheat the oven to 200°C/400°F/ Gas 6. Place the whole onions on a baking tray and cook for 35-45 minutes, or until they have some give but are still slightly firm. You don't want them to become mushy and lose their colour. Remove from the oven and cool a little. Peel and cut the onions as before and place on a baking tray under a hot grill or on a hot griddle pan and leave until lightly charred.

To serve, transfer the onions whilst still warm to a bowl, pour over the dressing, season with a little salt and pepper and mix gently but make sure the onions are well coated. Sprinkle with the pomegranate seeds and mint.

BROAD BEANS WITH JAMÓN

Broad beans are a delicacy in all their stages of growth: soft pods (up to 7cm long), steamed whole for 15-20 minutes, have a unique texture and taste. Really small beans can be eaten raw or simmered for 2-3 minutes until sweet. Medium-sized beans can be boiled for quite a long time (6-8 minutes) until they lose some of their tannic flavour and become sweet, or peeled. The skin of large broad beans can also be peeled and the beans enjoyed raw, or blanched for 1 minute before peeling. Always blanch them in unsalted water.

Serves 4
250g podded fresh broad beans, ideally thumbnail size
3 tablespoons extra virgin olive oil
juice of ½ lemon
2 tablespoons finely shredded mint
4 very thin slices of jamón (60g), preferably ibérico
   (pages 49 and 281)

Bring a saucepan of unsalted water to the boil, add the broad beans and blanch for 2-3 minutes or until tender, depending on their size. Strain in a colander and place under a running cold tap to cool down quickly. If the broad beans are large, peel off their pale skins. Place the beans in a bowl with the olive oil, lemon juice and mint, then season with a little salt and pepper to taste. Transfer the broad beans to a plate, lay the jamón slices on top and serve straight away.

PEAS, JAMÓN AND ANISE

We like to think that the food we cook is unaffected by fashion or fad, yet we are continually falling in love with new flavours and probably overusing them furiously. Green aniseed is one of those recent love affairs. Just biting on a seed makes one happy. We use it as a background flavour in many Spanish dishes, but it goes particularly well with peas. At Morito, we use a sweet Spanish aniseed liqueur called Anis del Mono; however, you could use a splash of Greek ouzo instead, if it is lurking in the drinks cabinet.

Serves 4
4 tablespoons olive oil
1 red onion, finely diced
2 spring onions, finely chopped
2 medium carrots, finely diced
1 garlic clove, thinly sliced
2 bay leaves, preferably fresh
1 sprig of thyme, leaves chopped
50g jamón ibérico (pages 49 and 281), cut into matchsticks
2 teaspoons green aniseed (page 280) or fennel seeds
300g frozen peas or petit pois
400ml vegetable stock or water
a splash of aniseed liqueur or ouzo
1 tablespoon shredded mint

Place a large pan over a medium heat and add the olive oil. When it is hot, add the onion, spring onion, carrots, garlic, bay leaves and thyme and cook gently for a few minutes, stirring occasionally. Add the jamón (if using) and aniseed or fennel seeds and continue to cook for about 10 minutes, stirring often, until the vegetables begin to soften. Add the peas and stock or water and bring to the boil. Lower the heat, season with salt and pepper and add the aniseed liqueur or ouzo. Simmer for 5 more minutes, then remove from the heat and stir in the mint. Serve with hot toast rubbed with garlic and drizzled with olive oil.

[vegetables]

PEAS, GEM LETTUCE AND SWEET HERBS

When braised, Little Gem lettuce has a pleasingly mild bitter taste that contrasts well with the sweetness of the peas and the herbs.

Serves 4

3 tablespoons olive oil, plus extra to serve

2 garlic cloves, thinly sliced, plus 1 garlic clove crushed
   to a paste with ½ teaspoon salt

a pinch of ground allspice

250g frozen peas or petit pois

2 tablespoons strained Greek yoghurt, such as Total, thinned
   with 1 tablespoon milk

2 Little Gem lettuces

½ teaspoon sugar

a squeeze of lemon

zest and juice of 1 orange

½ bunch of tarragon, chopped

½ bunch of dill, chopped

leaves from a few sprigs of mint, shredded

Place a saucepan over a medium heat, add the olive oil and fry the garlic until golden, then add the allspice and peas. Almost cover the peas with water and simmer for 5 minutes; don't add any salt.

Meanwhile, combine the yoghurt with the crushed garlic and season with a tiny pinch of salt and pepper. To prepare the lettuces, slice off the bases so that the leaves fall apart. Discard any tough or blemished outer leaves and slice the larger leaves in half lengthways. Wash the leaves and shake dry.

When the peas are cooked, add the sugar, lemon juice, orange zest and juice, and season with salt and pepper. Add the herbs and lettuce and toss together. Simmer for 20 seconds, then transfer to a serving dish. Spoon over small dollops of the garlic yoghurt, drizzle with olive oil and serve immediately.

WILTED LETTUCE, CRISPY BACON AND SHERRY VINEGAR

At Morito we cook this dish in a wok; otherwise a large frying pan will do.

> **Serves 4**
>
> 1 large escarole, romaine or cos lettuce
>
> 4 tablespoons extra virgin olive oil
>
> 8 very thin rashers of streaky bacon or panceta ibérica (page 281) or Italian pancetta, whole or cut into 1cm pieces
>
> 2 tablespoons sherry vinegar (page 280)
>
> ½ teaspoon sugar
>
> ½ garlic clove, crushed to a paste with a little salt

Trim off the tougher, darker leaves from the lettuce and discard. Wash the lettuce, dry well and cut into large bite-sized pieces.

Place a wok or large frying pan over a medium heat, add half the olive oil and fry the bacon or panceta until crisp. Remove from the heat, lift out the bacon, put aside and keep warm, reserving the oil in the pan.

Mix the vinegar, sugar, garlic, the remaining olive oil, salt and pepper together to make a dressing. When you are ready to eat, toss the lettuce with the dressing. Heat up the wok over a high heat with the bacon-flavoured oil. Add the lettuce and stir well for 30 seconds, or until the leaves just begin to wilt. Serve on a warm plate with the warm crispy bacon on top.

FRIED ARTICHOKES

It is best to make these when globe artichokes are in season during the spring and summertime. They make a delicious, salty accompaniment to a cold glass of sherry. We serve them with Alioli (page 161).

Serves 4
juice of ½ lemon
4 small-medium globe artichokes
1 litre sunflower oil, for deep-frying
100g plain flour
smoked Spanish paprika (page 280)
1 quantity of Alioli (page 161)
½ lemon, cut into wedges

To prepare the artichokes, fill a bowl with cold water and add the lemon juice. The general rule about artichokes is that whatever is green is tough, whatever is yellow is tender. Cut off the stalk from the base and peel 2-3mm off the remaining stalk. Snap off the green outer leaves until you get down to the leaves that are mostly yellow. Cut off the darker tips and peel the base until it too is yellow and tender. Scrape out all the furry choke from inside with a teaspoon. Cut each artichoke in quarters or sixths, depending on size, and place immediately in the lemony water. Just before cooking the artichokes, drain well, dry and toss with a generous pinch of salt.

Heat the oil in a large saucepan to about 180°C/350°F. Make sure that it does not come more than halfway up the pan, otherwise it may overflow when you add the artichokes. Coat the artichokes in the flour, gently tapping off any excess. Add them to the hot oil and fry until golden brown and tender, stirring regularly. Remove and place on kitchen paper to absorb any excess oil. Sprinkle with smoked paprika, and salt if needed. Serve immediately, with the alioli and lemon on the side.

ARTICHOKES, CHORIZO AND WHITE WINE

We appreciate that, for many people, preparing artichokes is a chore too far, and definitely not for those prone to arthritis. Having said that, we can't help thinking of Verona, a place we visit every time one of our books is published, as they are printed there (including this one). There is a lady in the shadow of the amphitheatre who appears to be in her eighties, and at certain times of year she prepares artichokes in their hundreds to sell them. So shame on you for hesitating to embark on this recipe.

Serves 4
3 tablespoons olive oil
150g cooking chorizo (page 281), diced into small pieces
3 medium globe artichokes, prepared (page 136) and each cut into sixths or eighths
1 teaspoon fennel seeds, roughly ground
1 garlic clove, thinly sliced
150ml white wine
150ml water
1 tablespoon shredded flat-leaf parsley or mint

Heat the olive oil in a pan over a medium heat. Add the chorizo and cook until crisp. Remove from the pan with a slotted spoon and put to one side. Add the artichokes, fennel seeds and garlic to the pan and cook for 1-2 minutes, stirring once or twice to prevent sticking. Now add the wine and water and cover with a lid. Cook the artichokes for about 10 minutes, then remove the lid and cook for a further 10 minutes or until tender. The liquid should have reduced. Remove from the heat, return the chorizo to the pan and check the seasoning. Serve with the parsley or mint scattered on top.

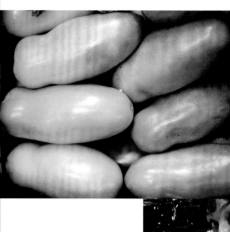

GREEN TOMATOES, CUMIN AND CRISPY GARLIC

This mezze is delicious with the Lebanese White Garlic Sauce opposite and sprinkled with sumac and mint.

Serves 4
150ml olive oil
4 garlic cloves, chopped into fine matchsticks
500g small green tomatoes, halved or quartered
1 tablespoon Forum Cabernet Sauvignon vinegar (page 280), or
   a good-quality aged red wine vinegar with a pinch of sugar
1 teaspoon cumin seeds, lightly toasted and ground (page 34)
a pinch of sugar
2 tablespoons shredded mint leaves
1 teaspoon sumac (page 280)
1 quantity of White Garlic Sauce (opposite)

Heat 100ml of the olive oil in a saucepan, add the garlic and fry over a medium heat until golden. Scoop out the garlic with a slotted spoon and put it on kitchen paper to absorb any excess oil. Replace the saucepan with a frying pan and strain 75ml of the oil into it. Turn up the heat to high and add the tomatoes. Fry until they begin to soften and are slightly coloured on both sides. Gently remove the delicate tomatoes from the pan.

To make the dressing, place the remaining 50ml olive oil, the vinegar, cumin, sugar and a good pinch of salt in a jar with a lid. Shake it until the dressing thickens a little. Pour over the warm tomatoes, sprinkle with the crispy garlic, mint and sumac and serve the white garlic sauce on the side.

WHITE GARLIC SAUCE

We discovered this Lebanese alioli in the Bekaa Valley during a wonderful lunch at the Massaya winery. Often served as part of a mezze, this sauce is delicious with chicken, fish or potatoes, or with fried green tomatoes (see opposite). The fresher and younger the garlic, the better.

Serves 4
2 heaped tablespoons cream cheese
1 tablespoon lemon juice
2 new-season garlic cloves (available from early spring, page 281), crushed to a smooth paste with ½ teaspoon salt
2 tablespoons sunflower oil
3 tablespoons extra virgin olive oil

Place the cream cheese and lemon juice in a bowl with 1 tablespoon of water and whisk to a smooth paste. Mix the garlic into the cream cheese, then vigorously whisk in the 2 oils, to create an emulsion.

GRILLED PEPPERS, PRESERVED LEMON AND CRISPY CAPERS

Red peppers will always have more flavour from early summer until the autumn. Romano peppers have been a revelation to us, because they have an additional intensity of sweetness, as well as a pleasingly thin flesh that is similar to the Spanish piquillo pepper. Good-quality tinned piquillo peppers can also be used in this recipe. We love this dish, not only because it looks fabulous but also because the flavours of the sweet peppers, preserved lemon and capers go brilliantly together.

Serves 4

3-4 Romano peppers (page 280), or piquillo peppers (page 280)

3 tablespoons extra virgin olive oil

½ garlic clove, crushed to a paste with a little salt

½ teaspoon cumin seeds, roughly ground

1-2 tablespoons Forum Cabernet Sauvignon vinegar (page 280), or a good-quality aged red wine vinegar with a pinch of sugar

1 tablespoon finely chopped preserved lemon rind (page 280)

1 quantity of Crispy Capers (page 27)

1 tablespoon finely shredded flat-leaf parsley

Blister and char the peppers over charcoal, under the grill or directly over a gas flame. Place in a bowl and cover with cling film. When cool enough to handle, peel off the skins and discard the seeds and stalks. Mix the olive oil, garlic, cumin and vinegar together, add the peppers, season with a little salt and pepper and marinate for 1-4 hours.

Lay the peppers on a plate and sprinkle the preserved lemon, capers and parsley on top.

BABA GHANOUSH

Traditionally a barbecue is essential for baba ghanoush, as the charcoal gives the aubergines a special smokiness. However, roasting them in the oven is still delicious. The skill with baba ghanoush is achieving that perfect balance between the tahini, lemon, olive oil and garlic. Quantities are a fairly accurate guide but taste is the best judge of all.

Serves 4
4 medium aubergines
2 tablespoons tahini
juice of 1 lemon
4 tablespoons extra virgin olive oil
1 garlic clove, crushed to a paste with ½ teaspoon salt
seeds of ½ pomegranate

If you are using a barbecue, grill the aubergines on all sides until the skins become black and almost crisp and the flesh is soft. This should take 15-20 minutes. Make sure you don't over-grill the aubergines, or you will be left with hardly any flesh when you peel them. Remove and let them cool.

If you are using the oven, preheat it to 240°C/475°F/Gas 9. Make a few incisions in the aubergines, to prevent them exploding in the oven, then roast for 25-40 minutes or until soft. Cool slightly.

Discard the stalks and peel the aubergines, making sure you remove all the black skin. Chop the flesh roughly and transfer to a bowl, along with the tahini, lemon juice, olive oil and garlic. Season with a good pinch of salt and mix well with a whisk or by hand until almost smooth. Taste and serve with the pomegranate seeds on top, and Flatbread (page 10).

FRIED AUBERGINES

Fried aubergines find their way on to the Morito menu in many seasonal guises:
with salmorejo (thick gazpacho) (below), miel de caña (cane molasses)
(page 146), pomegranate molasses and Spiced Labneh (page 91).

Serves 4
1-2 aubergines, sliced into rounds 1cm thick
150ml olive oil
150ml sunflower oil

Place the sliced aubergines in a colander, toss with a teaspoon of fine salt
and leave for 30 minutes to get rid of excess water and any bitterness.

Dry the aubergines on kitchen paper. Heat both oils in a wide frying pan
until hot but not smoking – about 180°C/350°F. Add the aubergine slices in a
single layer (in batches if necessary) and fry until a deep golden brown and
crisp on both sides. Remove from the pan and place on kitchen paper to absorb
any excess oil.

SALMOREJO
400g very ripe, sweet tomatoes
½ small red onion, roughly chopped
½ green pepper, roughly chopped
40g breadcrumbs
1 tablespoon Forum Cabernet Sauvignon vinegar (page 280), or
    a good-quality aged red wine vinegar with a pinch of sugar
½ garlic clove, crushed to a paste with a little salt
150ml extra virgin olive oil
a few sprigs of mint, leaves finely shredded

Put the tomatoes, onion and pepper in a food processor (or hand-held blender)
and blitz until smooth. Pass the purée through a coarse sieve, discarding the
dry pulp. Return the purée to the food processor and add the breadcrumbs,
vinegar, garlic and a pinch of salt. Turn the processor on and very slowly
begin to drizzle in the olive oil. It's like making mayonnaise; you want
the purée and the olive oil to emulsify so it thickens and becomes lighter
in colour. Transfer the salmorejo to a bowl and check the seasoning. If the
tomatoes are not sweet enough, you may need to add a pinch of sugar. Chill.
Fry the aubergines as above. To serve, pour the salmorejo into a wide shallow
bowl, place the aubergines on top and sprinkle with the shredded mint. Eat
immediately.

MIEL DE CAÑA

Miel de caña is a sticky, black Moorish molasses made from sugarcane. A good substitute is equal parts of runny honey and black treacle, or the juice of 4 pomegranates reduced over a low heat to a dark crimson syrup.

Serves 4

100g chickpea (gram) flour, seasoned with ½ teaspoon fine salt and 1 teaspoon very finely chopped rosemary

4 tablespoons miel de caña (page 280) or 2 tablespoons each of black treacle and runny honey, mixed, or 4 tablespoons of pomegranate molasses (page 280)

seeds of 1 pomegranate

1 heaped tablespoon finely shredded mint

Salt and fry the aubergines as on page 145, coating them first in the seasoned chickpea flour. Place them on a plate and drizzle the miel de caña all over, followed by the pomegranate seeds and shredded mint. Eat immediately.

SPICED LABNEH

Serves 4

3 tablespoons Forum Cabernet Sauvignon vinegar (page 280), or a good-quality aged red wine vinegar with a pinch of sugar

2 tablespoons finely shredded mint, plus extra to serve

1 red chilli, deseeded and finely chopped, plus extra to serve

2 garlic cloves, sliced into thin matchsticks and fried in a little olive oil until golden brown

½ teaspoon black onion seeds

1 quantity of Spiced Labneh (page 91)

Salt and fry the aubergines as on page 145, but for this recipe we like to fry them a little darker than usual. Transfer to a dish and sprinkle over the red wine vinegar, mint, chilli and garlic. These aubergines improve if left to sit for 20 minutes or so.

To serve, spoon a small dollop of the spiced labneh on top of each aubergine slice and finish with a little extra mint, chilli and the black onion seeds.

CUCUMBER CHIPS AND DILL YOGHURT

The sliced cucumber is coated in a simple cornflour batter. Both the batter
and the cucumber have a wonderful crunch, though of a different nature.
Combined with the cool yoghurt, this makes an excellent mezze.

Serves 4

2 medium cucumbers

4 tablespoons chopped dill, plus extra sprigs to garnish

1 garlic clove, crushed to a paste with ½ teaspoon salt

1-2 green chillies, deseeded and finely chopped

4 tablespoons strained Greek yoghurt, such as Total

a squeeze of lemon

300ml sunflower, olive or rapeseed oil, for deep-frying

1 red chilli, deseeded and finely chopped

a sprinkling of black onion seeds

BATTER

4 tablespoons cornflour

2 tablespoons plain flour

1 teaspoon baking powder

100ml water

Place all the dry ingredients for the batter in a bowl. Make a well in the
centre and slowly pour in the water, smoothing out any lumps with your
fingertips. Keep on adding water until the batter is the consistency of single
cream. Cover the bowl and chill in the fridge for at least 20 minutes.

Meanwhile, using a potato peeler, take alternate strips of peel off the
cucumbers so they become stripy. Now slice the cucumbers in half lengthways,
then into 1cm-thick slices at an angle to produce elongated half-moons. Toss
the cucumber with ½ teaspoon of salt and 1 tablespoon of the chopped dill,
then cover and put in the fridge.

To make the dill yoghurt, mix the remaining dill with the garlic, green
chillies, yoghurt and lemon juice, and season with salt and pepper.

Heat the oil in a large frying pan. Dip each piece of cucumber in the
batter, allow the excess to drip back into the bowl, and carefully place the
cucumber in the hot oil (cook in batches, if necessary). When they are crisp
on one side, turn over to finish cooking. They should be golden and slightly
puffed up. Lift them out with a slotted spoon and place on kitchen paper to
absorb any excess oil. Transfer to a plate, strew with the extra sprigs of
dill and the dill yoghurt on the side, sprinkled with the red chilli and
black onion seeds. Eat as soon as possible, while still crisp and hot.

SLOW-COOKED LEEKS, YOGHURT AND WALNUTS

Lightly toasted walnuts are scattered over the top of these leeks for crunch.

Serves 4

25g butter

1 tablespoon olive oil

600-700g leeks, trimmed and sliced into thin discs

2 tablespoons finely shredded mint leaves

2 tablespoons walnuts or pine nuts, toasted

1 quantity of Chilli Butter (page 116)

STABILISED YOGHURT

200g strained Greek yoghurt, such as Total

1 organic or free-range egg yolk

2 teaspoons cornflour or plain flour

To cook the leeks, melt the butter with the olive oil in a small-medium pan. When bubbling and golden, add the leeks and half the mint and season with salt and pepper. Cook over a medium heat for about 15-20 minutes, stirring occasionally or until they are soft and sweet.

To make the stabilised yoghurt, place all the ingredients in a bowl and whisk until smooth. When the leeks are ready, pour the stabilised yoghurt on to the leeks and cook for a minute or two while stirring continuously. The leek and yoghurt mixture needs to heat up but not boil, as this may cause it to split. Check the seasoning and transfer to a plate. Pour over the warm chilli butter and scatter over the remaining mint and walnuts or pine nuts.

CARROT, CARAWAY AND FETA

Sometimes we taste a carrot and we want to weep. There are certain times of
the year when a carrot has a perfume, an intensity, sweetness and complexity,
that is quite incredible. For us, it is very annoying that carrots can't
always taste like that, yet we think buying organic does help the flavour
a great deal.

Serves 4
500g organic carrots, peeled
4 tablespoons extra virgin olive oil
2 teaspoons caraway seeds, lightly crushed
juice of 1 lemon
100g feta cheese
1 tablespoon shredded mint
½ teaspoon black onion seeds (optional)

Preheat the oven to 200°C/400°F/Gas 6. Chop the carrots into quarters
lengthways and then into small cubes. Scatter them over a baking tray then
add 2 tablespoons of the olive oil, half the caraway and some seasoning.
Toss well. Bake for 30-40 minutes or until soft and slightly dry. The carrots
should develop a chewy texture and an intense, sweet flavour.

Remove the carrots from the oven and place in a bowl. Add the remaining
olive oil and caraway seeds, plus the lemon juice, and mix well. Check the
seasoning. Transfer to a plate, crumble the feta cheese all over and sprinkle
with the mint and black onion seeds. Serve warm.

GREEN BEANS, TOMATO AND CINNAMON YOGHURT

If you slow-cook green beans, flat beans or unstringy runner beans in this manner, then quite frankly you will never have tasted anything so delicious. This ancient Mediterranean way of cooking beans brings out their natural sweetness, but just as important is the incredible texture.

Serves 4
200ml olive oil
250g spring onions, including the green part, finely chopped
400g sweet tomatoes, roughly chopped
2 garlic cloves, chopped
3 bay leaves, preferably fresh
½ teaspoon baharat (page 280) or ground allspice
½ teaspoon ground cinnamon
a pinch of sugar
70ml white wine
500g green beans, trimmed and cut in half
200ml water or enough to cover the beans
2 tablespoons coriander leaves

CINNAMON YOGHURT
8 tablespoons strained Greek yoghurt, such as Total
½ teaspoon freshly ground cinnamon
½ garlic clove, crushed to a paste with a little salt

Heat the olive oil in a pan over a low heat and add the spring onions, tomatoes, garlic and bay leaves. Cook gently for a few minutes. Add the spices, sugar and a pinch of salt and continue cooking for 5 minutes. Add the wine, beans and the water and mix everything together. Cover with a lid and cook over a low heat, stirring occasionally, for 45 minutes to 1 hour, or until the beans have become very soft and the sauce has thickened. Check the beans every so often to ensure that they have enough liquid and are not sticking to the base of the pan.

Make the cinnamon yoghurt by mixing all the ingredients in a bowl. When the beans are ready, transfer to a large plate, drizzle with the cinnamon yoghurt and scatter the coriander leaves over the top. Serve with warm bread to mop up the juices.

PINK FIR APPLE AND FETA SALAD

The real star potato variety for this salad is Pink Fir Apple. A crazy name and a very particular potato, its characteristics are dense, earthy and dry. Pink Firs are available at posh veg shops, supermarkets and farmers' markets during the summer and autumn. If you can't get hold of them, use a variety of new potato instead.

Serves 4
400-500g potatoes, such as Pink Fir Apple, Charlotte or Ratte
4 large sprigs of mint
100g feta cheese, thinly sliced
5 tablespoons extra virgin olive oil
a pinch of dried oregano (optional)
3 spring onions, including the green part, sliced into thin rounds

Simmer the potatoes in well-salted water with 1 sprig of mint for 20-25 minutes or until tender. (Other varieties of potato may take less time to cook as they are less dense.) Drain the potatoes and discard the mint.

While the potatoes are cooling, pick the leaves off the remaining sprigs of mint and shred them finely. When the potatoes are just cool enough to handle, slice them into 8mm-thick rounds. Toss all the ingredients gently in a bowl. Have a quick taste to see if the seasoning needs adjusting. This salad can be eaten either hot or at room temperature. Delicious with Lamb Chops Mechoui (page 220) and chopped olives.

PATATAS ALIÑADAS

In Seville, very close to the cathedral, is a tapas bar called Casablanca. We had heard from locals over the years that their aliñadas were something special. A few months before Morito opened, we rocked up and ordered a beer, a fino and the greatly anticipated potatoes. It is magic when something so simple becomes something so divine. We walked away happy, yet also a bit sad. We knew that we could never replicate the combination of their potatoes, vinegar and oil, but we learnt enough from our Casablanca visit to ensure that our version is probably the best potato salad you are ever likely to eat in London. At Morito we use a mixture of Moscatel, Cabernet Sauvignon and sherry vinegars in equal parts (page 280). This dish is superb topped with good-quality tinned tuna (page 281), Alioli (page 161) and plenty of parsley.

Serves 4
4 medium (Cyprus) potatoes (about 750g), unpeeled
½ green pepper, very finely chopped
½ small red onion, very finely chopped
2 tablespoons Forum Cabernet Sauvignon vinegar (page 280), or
 a mixture as above, or a good-quality aged red wine vinegar
 with a pinch of sugar
175ml extra virgin olive oil, preferably a fruity one
1 tablespoon finely chopped flat-leaf parsley
smoked sweet Spanish paprika (page 280)

Add the whole potatoes to a saucepan of cold water with 2 teaspoons of salt added, bring to the boil and simmer for about 30 minutes or until soft. In the meantime, place the green pepper, onion and vinegar in a bowl and put to one side. Remove the potatoes from the pan and leave in a colander for 10 minutes to dry out a little.

While the potatoes are still hot, peel them and place in a bowl with the olive oil. Mash them with a potato masher, the back of a fork or even your hands; make sure you don't mash them to a fine purée, as some texture is desirable for this dish. It is important to mash the potatoes with the oil while they are warm, as they will absorb it much better.

Add the pepper, onion and vinegar mixture, combine and check the seasoning. Spread the mixture on a plate, sprinkle with the chopped parsley and a little paprika and serve, ideally with *picos*, the Andalucían breadsticks (page 281).

WRINKLED POTATOES WITH MOJO VERDE

Traditionally the potatoes for this Canary Island classic are cooked in
seawater and the exotic variety used is every shade of purple and red, partly
due to the volcanic soil they are grown in. The evaporation technique for
cooking potatoes is so easy and the results so unusual, that we now find
ourselves turning to it for the everyday cooking of small potatoes.

Serves 4

500g small new potatoes, such as Jersey Royals, washed

about 300ml water

1 quantity of Mojo Verde (below)

Place the whole, unpeeled potatoes in a medium saucepan in a single layer.
Add 2 teaspoons of salt and the water, so the potatoes are covered two-thirds
of the way up. Bring to the boil and cover with a disc of greaseproof paper,
tucked snugly around the potatoes. Simmer over a low-medium heat for 20-30
minutes or until the water has evaporated fully. Lift off the greaseproof
paper and continue to cook for a couple of minutes, until the bottom of the
potatoes are a little bit black and blistered, they have a white coating of
salt and are slightly wrinkled. Serve with the mojo verde, scooping it up
with the warm potatoes.

MOJO VERDE

Serves 4

1 large bunch of coriander, roughly chopped

8 green chillies, deseeded (only if hot) and roughly chopped

1 garlic clove, sliced

200ml extra virgin olive oil

juice of 1 lemon

**1 tablespoon sweet white wine vinegar, such as Moscatel (page
    280) or ordinary white wine vinegar with a pinch of sugar**

Put the coriander, chillies, garlic and half the olive oil in a food
processor and blitz until smooth. Transfer to a bowl and add the remaining
oil with the lemon juice and vinegar. Season with salt and stir well.

PATATAS BRAVAS

Only recently have we started to serve patatas bravas with a generous dollop of alioli. Goodness knows why we haven't done it before — it's a classic.

Serves 4

BRAVAS SAUCE
4 tablespoons olive oil
2 garlic cloves, finely chopped
1 tablespoon finely chopped rosemary
1 sprig of thyme, leaves chopped
2 bay leaves, preferably fresh
2 dried bird's eye chillies, crumbled
3 tablespoons red wine
400g tin of plum tomatoes, blitzed
a pinch of sugar
a pinch of smoked hot Spanish paprika
   (page 280)
a pinch of smoked sweet Spanish paprika
   (page 280)

POTATOES
750g potatoes, peeled and chopped roughly
   into 2cm cubes
1 litre sunflower, rapeseed or olive oil
1 quantity of Alioli, to serve (opposite)

For the bravas sauce, heat the oil in a saucepan over a medium heat, add the garlic, rosemary, thyme, bay leaves and chillies and fry gently until you begin to smell the aromas from the herbs. Add the wine and tomatoes, season with salt, then add the sugar and both paprikas. Cook the sauce over a medium-high heat for 15-20 minutes. You want it to reduce a little to concentrate the flavour, but you don't want to make it too rich. Take it off the heat and check the seasoning.

Mix the potatoes with 1 teaspoon of salt and leave in a colander for 20 minutes. Pour the oil into a deep-fat fryer or a large saucepan. Remember to fill the saucepan only halfway up with the oil. Heat it until hot but not smoking, 180-200°C/350-400°F. Use a frying basket or slotted spoon to lower the potatoes into the hot oil. Fry for a few minutes, stirring once, until golden and crisp on the outside and soft inside. Remove from the hot oil and place in a bowl lined with kitchen paper to absorb the excess oil. Serve immediately, with the bravas sauce on top and a big dollop of alioli.

ALIOLI

Morito alioli is less strong and therefore more versatile than recipes of old.

Serves 4

100ml extra virgin olive oil

100ml sunflower oil

2 large organic or free-range egg yolks

1 teaspoon Dijon mustard

1-2 garlic cloves, crushed to a smooth paste with ½ teaspoon
   salt

a splash of sweet white wine vinegar such as Moscatel (page
   280), or ordinary white wine vinegar with a pinch of sugar

juice of ½ lemon

Mix the olive and sunflower oils in a jug. Place the egg yolks, mustard and
1 teaspoon of water in a bowl and start blending with a hand-held blender,
or by hand with a balloon whisk. Very slowly but constantly, begin to add
the oil and do not stop whisking until it has all been incorporated and the
mixture is thick and pale yellow. Add the garlic, vinegar and lemon juice to
taste, then check the seasoning. If you want to make this beforehand, the
mayonnaise (without the garlic) will keep, covered, for a couple of days in
the fridge; just add the garlic before serving.

FISH

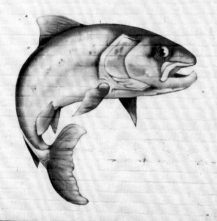

SHELL FISH

HADDOCK   ROLL MOPS
        P I E C E S
        S A L M O N
AND   SATURDAY
        M A R K E T
L   O   C   A   L

SEA BASS CEVICHE, SEVILLE ORANGE AND CUMIN

Ceviche is a class dish. The fish is eaten raw, but in fact it does 'cook' (change colour and texture) with the help of the acid in the citrus fruit. We were desperate to include ceviche in our repertoire so, to give the dish a Moorish slant, we use Seville oranges when in season from early January, as well as cumin. Bergamot oranges can be substituted for Seville oranges if you wish, or lemon with a touch of orange zest to finish. We often use raw scallops and raw prawns instead of sea bass or a mixture of all three. The common factor, however, is that they must be super-fresh.

Serves 4

120g filleted sea bass, or
    scallops (halved in discs)
    and/or prawns, left whole
juice of 2 Seville (page 281)
    or Bergamot oranges, or of
    1 orange and 1 lemon
a pinch of dried oregano
a pinch of sugar
1 teaspoon sweet white wine
    vinegar such as Moscatel
    (page 280), or ordinary
    white wine vinegar with a
    pinch of sugar

finely grated zest of ½
    (Seville, Bergamot or
    normal) orange
a pinch of toasted cumin
    seeds, ground (page 34)
½ spring onion, including
    the pale green part, very
    thinly sliced
a drizzle of extra virgin
    olive oil

With your favourite sharp knife, slice the sea bass paper-thin, either directly down or slightly at an angle, as if you were slicing smoked salmon. Cover each plate with a layer of the fish, or with the scallops or prawns, if using. (If the fish is not quite thin enough, you can flatten it a little bit more with the flat side of your knife.) This can be done up to 3 hours in advance, if you cover the fish in cling film and put it in the fridge.

Ten minutes before you are ready to eat, mix the citrus juice, oregano, sugar, a good pinch of salt and the vinegar together and check the seasoning. Spoon the juice evenly over the fish, lifting up the fish on the plate so the underside gets a little bit of the marinade as well as the top. Leave to marinate for 3-5 minutes, depending on how thinly your sea bass is sliced and your own personal taste; 3 minutes is medium-rare; 5 minutes is well done.

Now the finishing touches: grate the orange zest directly on to the fish as evenly as possible. Sprinkle over the cumin and spring onion, drizzle with olive oil, then serve straight away.

SALT COD, BROAD BEANS AND MINT

When soaking salt cod overnight, rinse the fish a few times beforehand
otherwise it may still be unbearably salty, especially as it is eaten raw in
this dish. To judge the saltiness, taste a pinch from the centre. Blanched
podded and peeled broad beans are also delicious.

Serves 4
100g medium-cured salt cod fillet (page 281), rinsed well,
**   then soaked in cold water in the fridge overnight or longer**
250g podded fresh broad beans, ideally thumbnail size
3-4 tablespoons extra virgin olive oil
a few sprigs of mint, finely shredded
juice and zest of ½ lemon
100g rocket (optional)

Drain the salt cod, remove any bones and shred the flesh. Bring a saucepan
of unsalted water to the boil and blanch the broad beans for a couple of
minutes, until tender, depending on their size. Drain in a colander and cool
under running water. If the broad beans are large, peel off their pale outer
skins. Put the beans in a bowl with the salt cod, olive oil, mint, lemon
juice, zest and rocket (if using). Season with salt and pepper, checking for
salt first as the cod is already salty.

SALT COD CROQUETAS

If you are using salt cod that is hard as a board and designed to sail to the Americas and back unscathed, then change the overnight soaking water in the morning and give it a few more hours. This Portuguese recipe is hard to beat. If it were a Spanish version, béchamel sauce would be used instead of potato, although in some parts of Galicia potato might still be used.

Makes 12-16 croquetas / serves 4
**250g hard or medium-cured salt cod fillet (page 281), rinsed
  well, then soaked in cold water in the fridge overnight
  or longer**
1 small red onion, halved
3 bay leaves, preferably fresh
750ml whole milk
2 potatoes (about 350g), peeled and quartered
1½ tablespoons finely shredded flat-leaf parsley
750ml-1 litre sunflower oil, for deep-frying
1 quantity of Alioli (page 161)
½ lemon, cut into wedges

Drain the salt cod and place in a saucepan with one half of the red onion, bay leaves and milk. Gently bring to a simmer, but remove the cod from the pan before it comes to the boil.

Add the potatoes to the pan. Simmer until just soft. Meanwhile, finely shred the fish, removing any bones and skin. This is much easier to do when it is still hot; try to break down the fibres as much as possible. When the potatoes are ready, drain in a colander, then leave them spread out to dry for 3 minutes and mash until smooth. Finely grate the remaining half of red onion and mix 1 heaped tablespoon of it with the potato, parsley and the shredded salt cod while still warm. Using 2 dessertspoons, shape the mixture into oval quenelles, cover and chill in the fridge.

Heat the oil in a deep-fat fryer or a large saucepan, ensuring it does not reach more than halfway up the sides. When it reaches about 180°C/350°F, or when a test piece of the salt cod mixture sizzles furiously in the oil, fry the croquetas, in 2 batches, until golden brown and crunchy. Carefully transfer them to kitchen paper to drain. Serve hot with the alioli and lemon on the side.

PESCAITO FRITO (FRIED FISH)

Eating deep-fried fish is one of life's great pleasures, especially with a glass of chilled fino in hand. Andalucía is the best place for fried fish, and we have often puzzled over how they do it so well. Here are our observations:

- Use olive oil, or half sunflower oil and half olive oil, to fry fish, as it does make a difference to the flavour.
- Use half plain flour and half fine semolina flour, or fish frying flour (page 281) to dust the fish.
- Salt the fish well and leave for a minute or two before you are ready to coat and fry it. This should draw out a little of the moisture and therefore help the flour stick to the fish prior to frying.
- Deep-frying fish is really quite an investment. To do it well, you need 2-3 litres of oil. If you skimp on the amount of oil, the temperature will drop too much when the fish is added. The flour then has time to absorb the oil and become greasy. For the same reason, don't try to cook too much fish at once. In small batches is better.
- The oil needs to be pretty darned hot − about 200°C/400°F.
- Once the fish is cooked, don't hang around to eat it. Fried fish will become less crisp by the second.
- For future frying, once the oil has cooled, carefully strain through a fine sieve into a jar. With a bit of topping up, you can reuse it 3 or 4 times.

> **Serves 4**
> 100g fish per person: squid (prepared as on page 198 and cut into rings), puntillitas (baby squid) or any small fresh fish such as anchovies, red mullet, or a mixture
> 2-3 litres olive oil, or a mixture of sunflower and olive oil
> 125g plain flour or fish frying flour (page 281)
> 125g fine semolina
> ½ tablespoon sumac (optional)
> 1 lemon, cut into quarters
> 1 quantity of Alioli (page 161)

Wash the squid or puntillitas and pat dry. Scale and gut any small fish, if necessary, and wash well, or fillet and cut up if big. Season the squid and/or fish generously with salt, including inside the bellies for whole fish.

Pour the oil into a deep-fat fryer or a very large saucepan; it should come no more than halfway up the sides. Heat to about 200°C/400°F. Meanwhile, mix the flour and semolina together. Toss the squid and/or fish in it and dust off any excess. Fry in the hot oil in 2 batches for 1-2 minutes, depending on size, until golden and crisp. If the (whole) fish are large, reduce the heat a little so they will be cooked inside while crisp on the outside. Remove from the pan; place in a bowl lined with kitchen paper to drain off excess oil. Sprinkle with the sumac if using. Serve immediately, with lemon and alioli.

GAMBAS ROJAS A LA PLANCHA

At Morito, we use Spanish red prawns, as the colour, flavour and texture are absolutely spectacular. They have a vibrant red shell even when raw, a sweet flavour and a soft, smooth texture that melts in the mouth. However, red prawns are not the easiest to come by, so if you can't get hold of them, ask your fishmonger for another type of raw prawn. We serve the prawns with Avocado Mojo (below), Mojo Verde (page 158) or Alioli (page 161).

Serves 4

AVOCADO MOJO

1 large bunch of coriander, washed and roughly chopped

2 small garlic cloves

4-6 green chillies, halved lengthways and deseeded

100ml extra virgin olive oil

1 ripe, creamy avocado, peeled, pitted and chopped small

2 tablespoons lemon juice

1 tablespoon sweet white wine vinegar, such as Moscatel
   (page 280), or white wine vinegar with a pinch of sugar

PRAWNS

a drizzle of olive oil

12–16 red prawns (page 281)

1 lemon, cut into quarters

Put the coriander, garlic, chillies and olive oil in a food processor and blend until smooth. Transfer to a bowl, stir in the avocado and season with the lemon juice, vinegar and salt to taste.

To cook the prawns, heat a frying pan or plancha over a medium to high heat, then drizzle with a little olive oil and add the prawns. Season with salt and cook for a few seconds on each side. Serve immediately with the mojo or alioli and lemon.

PRAWNS, TAMARIND AND GREEN CHILLI

We are ashamed to say that we cannot remember where this recipe came from, and therefore what tenuous link with Moorish culture or the Eastern Mediterranean it has. We love tamarind, and if you are unfamiliar with cooking with it, this is a good place to start. Please use dried blocks of tamarind, as other more processed forms can have a strange taste.

Serves 4
500g raw or cooked North Atlantic prawns (page 281), shell-on
60g dried tamarind, crumbled into small pieces
20g butter
2 tablespoons olive oil
3 garlic cloves, finely sliced
¾ teaspoon ground coriander seeds
1-2 green chillies, deseeded and finely chopped
1 teaspoon sugar
1 tablespoon roughly chopped coriander leaves

Peel the prawns, then place the shells in a small saucepan, just cover with water and bring to the boil. Simmer for 5 minutes, mushing the shells a bit to extract more flavour, then strain. Put the tamarind in a bowl and pour over the hot prawn stock. When the tamarind is cool enough to handle, squish the pulp with your fingertips to loosen it from the seeds. Push the pulp through a sieve with a rubber spatula.

In a saucepan over a medium heat, melt the butter in the olive oil. Fry the garlic until it starts to colour, then add the ground coriander and the chillies. Cook for 30 seconds, and add the prawn and tamarind stock. Simmer until the sauce starts to thicken a little, then season with the sugar, salt and pepper.

If using raw prawns, cook them in the sauce for a minute or so. If they are cooked, remove the pan from the heat and stir in the prawns, just so they heat through. Sprinkle over the chopped coriander and serve.

PRAWNS, SPINACH AND HARISSA

If you are using bought harissa, then add only 2 teaspooons and increase the amount of lemon juice to give that extra freshness.

Serves 4
400g spinach
300g cooked North Atlantic prawns (page 281), peeled
5 tablespoons extra virgin olive oil
juice of 1 lemon
1 tablespoon Harissa (page 176)
a pinch of sugar
a few coriander leaves

Bring a large saucepan of salted water to the boil and blanch the spinach in it for a minute. Drain in a colander and refresh under cold running water. Give the spinach a good squeeze to get rid of excess water, transfer to a bowl and add all the remaining ingredients except the coriander leaves. Mix well, season with a little salt and check the seasoning. Scatter the coriander leaves on top.

HARISSA

In every book that we have written there has been a recipe for harissa, and in every book it has been different. Each family has its own version of harissa and this is Morito's version. We add rare black cumin seeds, which makes it unique. The reason we incorporate this unconventional spice is that our local shop, Rima's (four doors away from Morito), has always stocked it. We found it gave a wonderfully smoky, ethereal quality to the flavour and we have never looked back. It is great to nibble on with Flatbread (page 10).

Serves 8
250g red chillies, halved lengthways and deseeded
1 garlic clove, crushed to a paste with ½ teaspoon salt
100g piquillo peppers (page 280)
2 tablespoons caraway seeds, lightly toasted and ground
1½ tablespoons cumin seeds, lightly toasted and ground
  (page 34)
½ tablespoon black cumin seeds, ground (optional) (page 280)
4 tablespoons extra virgin olive oil
1 teaspoon smoked sweet Spanish paprika (page 280)
2 tablespoons Forum Cabernet Sauvignon vinegar (page 280), or
  a good-quality aged red wine vinegar with a pinch of sugar

Put the chillies and 1 teaspoon of salt in a food processor and blend until very smooth. Add the garlic, piquillo peppers, caraway, cumin and black cumin, if using, and blitz until very smooth again.

Transfer to a bowl and add the olive oil, followed by the paprika, so it dissolves into the oil and turns it red. Add the vinegar, stir well and season to taste with salt. Harissa can be stored in a sealed jar in the fridge for up to 2 weeks.

TORTILLITAS

No, not tortillas. Tortillitas are crisp fritters made with chickpea flour. Prawn and shrimp tortillitas turn really crisp, crab ones less so, but they are still completely delicious. Sanlúcar de Barrameda on Andalucía's Atlantic coast is the home of tortillitas, as well as of the wonderful manzanilla sherry. Drink up, eat these little morsels and prepare to be transported to Sanlúcar's shoreline.

Makes 8 biscuit-sized tortillitas

BATTER

50g chickpea (gram) flour

100ml soda water

⅓ teaspoon bicarbonate of soda

1 teaspoon finely chopped flat-leaf parsley

SEAFOOD

120g peeled raw or cooked prawns, finely sliced, or 120g
  peeled brown shrimps, or 120g white crab meat

200-300ml olive oil, for frying

lemon wedges

Put the chickpea flour into a small bowl and add half the soda water. Using your fingertips, mix the flour and water together, smoothing out the lumps as you go. When smooth, add the rest of the soda water, the bicarbonate of soda, parsley and a pinch of salt. When you are ready to eat, stir in the seafood and check the seasoning. Line a baking tray with kitchen paper and turn your oven to low if you want to keep the first batch of tortillitas warm.

Heat a large non-stick frying pan over a medium to high heat and pour in enough olive oil to cover the bottom of the pan by 5mm. When the oil is hot, take a heaped dessertspoon of the mixture, marginally tilt the pan so the oil pools on one side, then put the mixture on the dry side of the pan. With the pan still tilted, spread out the mixture as thinly as possible, making little pecking actions with your spoon to try to encourage small holes to appear in the tortillita. (The idea is that when you tilt the oil back in the other direction it fills up the tiny holes, making it crisp all the way through.) Depending on the size of your pan, there should be space for three more tortillitas. After you have put the fourth spoonful in the pan, it should be time to turn over your first. The colour should be dark golden, but be warned that chickpea flour can become unpleasantly bitter if allowed to turn dark brown. Don't worry if the tortillitas touch in the pan, as they are quite easy to separate using a spatula and spoon.

Transfer the tortillitas to the lined baking tray, remove any debris from the pan and top up with more oil before cooking the next. Either keep warm in the oven or eat straight away with the lemon and a glass of manzanilla.

Butterflied —

25 BREM
30 LEGS
20 BASS
5 BASS Fil
12 PORTION CR
2 L. SCALOPS
5 L. CATFISH

SCALLOPS A LA PLANCHA

We are spoilt with the wonderful diver-caught scallops we get from the east
coast of Scotland. A juicy scallop on the plancha is pretty hard to beat.
The only dilemma is which sauce to choose (see below). If not using the
sauces immediately, do not store them in the fridge as they will set and
never regain their texture. They will keep well out of the fridge for up to
8 hours.

Serves 4

SHERRY BUTTER SAUCE

75ml sherry vinegar (page 280)

75ml fino sherry

1 tablespoon sugar

4 black peppercorns

2 bay leaves, preferably fresh

125g unsalted butter, cut into cubes and kept in the fridge

Place the vinegar, fino, sugar, peppercorns and bay leaves in a saucepan over
a medium heat and simmer until it becomes thick and syrupy and has reduced
to about 4 tablespoons. Remove from the heat, discard the bay leaves and
peppercorns and cool. Return the pan to a very low heat, or a bain-marie.
Begin to add the butter gradually, whisking all the time. As you add more and
more butter, the sauce will begin to look velvety and lighter in colour. When
all the butter has been incorporated, it should be the colour of honey and
the consistency of double cream. Serve warm.

ALBARIÑO BUTTER SAUCE

125g unsalted butter

5 spring onions, very finely chopped

150ml albariño wine, from Galicia

Melt the butter in a small pan over a medium heat. Add the spring onions with
a good pinch of salt and a little pepper and cook gently for 5-10 minutes
until they become soft. Add the wine and simmer for 5-10 minutes. Check for
seasoning. Serve warm.

SEVILLE ORANGE BUTTER SAUCE

juice of 3 Seville oranges (available in early January)
    (page 281) or 2 oranges and 1 lemon

finely grated zest of ½ orange

1 sprig of thyme

1 bay leaf, preferably fresh

5 black peppercorns

1½ teaspoons sugar

100g unsalted butter, cut into cubes and kept in the fridge

Place the citrus juice, zest, thyme, bay leaf and peppercorns in a pan over a medium heat and simmer until reduced by half. Remove the thyme, bay and peppercorns, then add the sugar and a good pinch of salt and over a low heat slowly begin to add the cold butter, whisking constantly. When all the butter has been added, the sauce should have thickened and become velvety in texture. Remove from the heat.

THE SCALLOPS

- 6 medium scallops, cut in half horizontally
- 1 tablespoon olive oil

Place a wide frying pan or plancha over a high heat and season the scallops with salt. When the pan is hot, add the oil, followed by the scallops. Sear for 1-2 minutes on each side, until golden but not cooked through. Remove from the pan and serve with the chosen sauce.

SCALLOPS, TOMATO AND CHORIZO

Serves 4

3½ tablespoons extra virgin olive oil

1 tablespoon Forum Cabernet Sauvignon vinegar (page 280), or
  a good-quality aged red wine vinegar with a pinch of sugar

150g cooking chorizo (page 281), diced small

6 medium scallops, cut in half horizontally

12-15 cherry tomatoes, quartered

½ small red onion, finely chopped

1 tablespoon finely shredded flat-leaf parsley

First make the dressing. Whisk 2½ tablespoons of the olive oil with the
vinegar and some salt and pepper. Check the seasoning and set aside.

Heat a wide frying pan over a high heat, add the remaining tablespoon
of olive oil and, when hot, add the chorizo. Cook until crisp, then transfer
to a bowl with a slotted spoon and keep warm. With the pan still over a high
heat, quickly season the scallops with salt and pepper and sear briefly on
both sides until golden. Transfer to a bowl and mix in the tomatoes, onion,
chorizo and dressing. Sprinkle over the parsley and serve immediately.

RAZOR CLAMS AND SALPICÓN

Navajas are deliciously sweet razor clams (named for their resemblance to an old cut-throat razor). If you can't get hold of razor clams, plump mussels are also wonderful. Salpicón is a refreshing half dressing, half finely chopped salad that is great with all seafood.

Serves 4
8-12 razor clams, depending on size, or 20 mussels, cleaned
2 tablespoons olive oil
150g cooking chorizo (page 281), diced small (optional)

DRESSING
4 tablespoons extra virgin olive oil
1 tablespoon Forum Cabernet Sauvignon vinegar (page 280), or
   a good-quality aged red wine vinegar with a pinch of sugar

SALPICÓN
½ cucumber, peeled, deseeded and finely diced
½ red Romano pepper (page 280) or ½ small bell pepper, diced
½ small green pepper, finely diced
½ red onion, finely diced
1 red chilli, deseeded and finely chopped
200g cherry tomatoes, cut into eighths
2 tablespoons finely shredded flat-leaf parsley

Rinse the razor clams or mussels. Place a small pan over a medium-high heat, add 1 tablespoon of olive oil and fry the chorizo, if using, for a few minutes until it begins to crisp. Remove and keep warm.

To cook the razor clams or mussels, heat a large saucepan over a high heat, add the remaining tablespoon of olive oil, followed by the clams or mussels, and cover with a lid. Shake the pan for half a minute and remove from the heat as soon as the razor clams or mussels begin to open. Discard any that haven't opened. Cut off the sand pouch at one end from each razor clam with a pair of scissors. If the pouch breaks, just rinse the clam to get rid of any trapped sand.

To make the dressing, put the ingredients in a jam jar with a lid, season with salt and pepper and shake well. For the salpicón, put all the ingredients except ½ tablespoon of the chopped parsley in a bowl, pour on the dressing and toss well.

To serve, put the hot razor clams or mussels in their shells on to a plate, spoon over the salpicón, sprinkle with the warm chorizo, if using, and the remaining parsley.

GRILLED SARDINES, CORIANDER AND CUMIN

These sardines are at their most delicious when cooked over charcoal.

Serves 4
8 very fresh sardines, scaled and gutted
1 young garlic clove, finely chopped (page 281)
1½ teaspoons cumin seeds, toasted and roughly ground
**   (page 34)**
juice of 1 lemon
1 small bunch of coriander, leaves picked
1½ tablespoons finely chopped preserved lemon rind (page 280)
a drizzle of extra virgin olive oil
1 quantity of Harissa (page 176) (optional)

Salt the sardines generously. Heat a barbecue, a griddle pan or a heavy frying pan over a high heat and add the sardines. They need literally a couple of minutes on each side, just until the flesh turns opaque, so be careful not to overcook them. Bear in mind that they will continue to cook a little even after they are taken off the heat.

When ready, transfer to a plate and scatter all the remaining ingredients on top, finishing with the oil. Serve immediately with some harissa, if using, Morito bread and a cold beer.

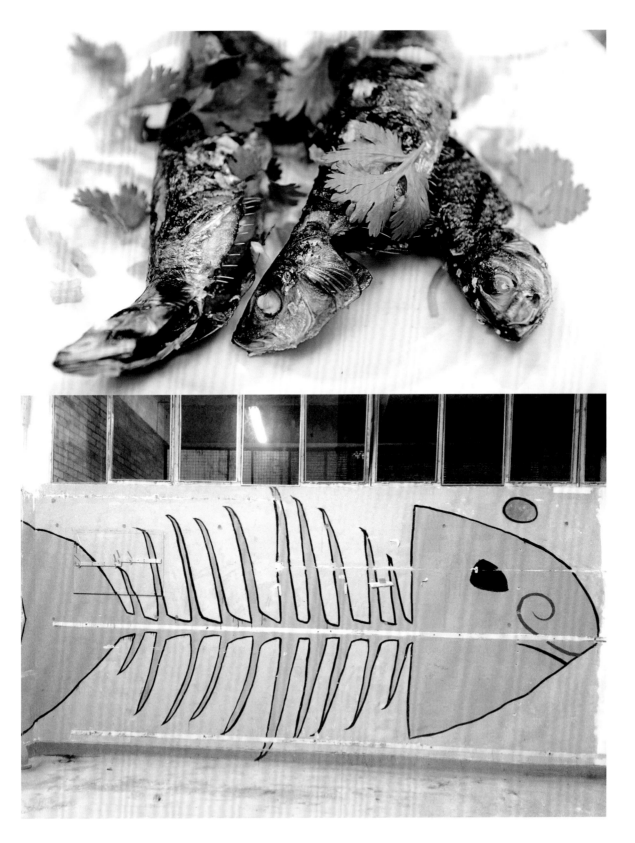

MACKEREL KEBABS, WALNUTS AND CHILLI

One of the great pleasures of visiting Istanbul is the food. At the foot of the Grand Bazaar sit a couple of bobbing boats selling fried mackerel with flatbread and pickles. Cheap and cheerful, yet so good, and a memory we will always cherish. Supermarket flatbread tends to be too thick or heavy. If possible, source an authentic brand, or make your own (page 10). This recipe is also delicious made with sardines, or barbecued fish. We bet it would be really delicious made with smoked mackerel as well.

Serves 4

4 heaped tablespoons shredded white cabbage

1 teaspoon caraway seeds, crushed

juice of ½ lemon

2 tablespoons extra virgin olive oil

2 tablespoons roughly chopped mint or flat-leaf parsley

2 tablespoons strained Greek yoghurt, such as Total

1 tablespoon whole milk or water

1 garlic clove, crushed to a paste with ½ teaspoon salt

3 teaspoons tahini

a small knob (25g) of butter

2 fresh mackerel fillets

2 Flatbreads (page 10), or pitta breads

1-2 red chillies, deseeded and chopped

4 pickled chillies (page 280)

1 tablespoon crushed walnuts

Dress the cabbage with the caraway, lemon juice, olive oil and mint or parsley. Season with salt and pepper and set aside. Mix the yoghurt, milk or water, garlic and tahini together and check the seasoning.

In a frying pan, melt the butter over a medium heat. Salt the mackerel and place skin-side up in the pan. Cook for 3 minutes on each side. Meanwhile toast the bread and, when hot, cut in half to create 4 pouches.

With a fork, flake the mackerel into small chunks, skin and all, and divide between the breads. Sprinkle the cabbage salad over the fish, then spoon on the yoghurt, followed by both the fresh and pickled chillies and the walnuts. Wrap the bread in a napkin and munch away.

OCTOPUS, TOMATOES, CAPERS AND DILL

We had this mezze in Beirut, with a glass of arak. Perfect.

Serves 4
1-1.25kg fresh or defrosted frozen octopus, preferably
  double-sucker
1 white onion, halved
3 bay leaves, preferably fresh
3 tablespoons extra virgin olive oil
250g cherry tomatoes, quartered
½ red onion, finely sliced
100g purslane (page 281) or rocket (optional)
2 tablespoons chopped dill, plus extra sprigs to serve
1 quantity of Crispy Capers (page 27)

DRESSING
10 cherry tomatoes, blitzed in a food processor
6 tablespoons extra virgin olive oil
½ teaspoon green aniseed (page 280) or fennel seeds, ground
1 tablespoon Forum Cabernet Sauvignon vinegar (page 280), or
  a good-quality aged red wine vinegar with a pinch of sugar
1 tablespoon arak, anise seco, pastis or ouzo

To prepare the octopus yourself, first slice its head, or 'hood', open and remove the gelatinous sac of guts from inside. Now remove the hard, black, beaky mouth, located at the centre where the 8 tentacles meet. Place the octopus in a large saucepan and add the onion, bay leaves, olive oil and enough water to cover by about 5cm. Gently simmer the octopus for 45 minutes to 1 hour or until tender. To check if it is ready, insert a small skewer through the thickest part of a tentacle. When the skewer goes through the centre without finding rubbery resistance, it's done. Remove from the pot and drain in a colander. Slice the tentacles into thin discs and the head into strips, then place in a bowl and keep warm.

For the dressing, put all the ingredients into a jam jar with a lid, season with salt and pepper and give it a good shake.

Add the quartered tomatoes, red onion, purslane or rocket if using, and dill to the bowl with the octopus and pour over the dressing. Give the salad a good mix, check the seasoning and transfer to a serving dish. Sprinkle over the extra sprigs of dill and the crispy capers.

PULPO GALLEGO

Probably the most famous tapa from Galicia. Excellent olive oil and crunchy rock salt are essential for this dish.

Serves 4
1.25kg fresh or defrosted frozen octopus, preferably double-sucker
1 onion, halved
3 bay leaves, preferably fresh
8 tablespoons extra virgin olive oil
800g potatoes, peeled
¼ teaspoon smoked sweet Spanish paprika (page 280)
¼ teaspoon smoked hot Spanish paprika (page 280)
rock salt (page 281)

If the octopus hasn't already been prepared by your fishmonger, you will need to clean it. Follow the method on page 193, cooking it with the onion, bay leaves and 2 tablespoons of the olive oil. Remove the octopus from the pan, reserving the cooking water. Slice the tentacles into 1.5cm-thick discs, place in a bowl and keep warm.

Add the potatoes to the octopus cooking water and simmer for around 20-30 minutes or until just tender. Remove from the pot, drain and leave to dry for 5 minutes. Slice the potatoes into 1.5cm-thick discs, place in the centre of a warm plate and surround with the warm octopus. Drizzle the remaining olive oil over everything. Finally, sprinkle the paprika and some rock salt evenly on top. Serve while still warm.

OCTOPUS WITH POTATO AND BEAN PURÉE

Serves 4

1-1.25kg fresh or defrosted frozen octopus, preferably
  double-sucker

1 onion, halved

3 bay leaves, preferably fresh

2 tablespoons extra virgin olive oil, plus extra to serve

POTATO AND BEAN PURÉE

200g split fava (dried broad) beans (page 281), or red
  lentils

1.1 litres water

9 tablespoons extra virgin olive oil

½ white onion, roughly chopped

3 bay leaves, preferably fresh

400g potatoes, peeled and chopped into 1cm cubes

TO SERVE

½ red onion, very finely diced

1 small bunch of dill, roughly chopped

1 teaspoon cumin seeds, lightly toasted and ground (page 34)

a handful of olives (page 280)

½ lemon, cut into wedges

If the octopus hasn't already been prepared by your fishmonger, you will need to clean it. Follow the method on page 193, cooking it with the onion, bay leaves and olive oil. Slice the head in strips and the tentacles into 1.5cm-thick discs, place in a bowl and keep warm.

To make the potato and bean purée, rinse the beans, put them in a large saucepan with the water, 2 tablespoons of the olive oil, the onion and bay leaves and bring to the boil. Reduce the heat to medium and cook for around 35 minutes, stirring frequently, until the beans begin to soften and break up. Remember to skim off any white froth that appears on the top of the water. Add the potatoes to the pan and continue to cook for about 20–30 minutes, until the potatoes are soft and the mixture starts to look like a purée, mashing the potatoes if necessary. Stir frequently, as the thicker the mixture becomes, the more easily it can stick and burn. Stir in 6 tablespoons of olive oil and season generously with salt to taste. Cook for a further 5 minutes, then remove from the heat.

Transfer the purée to a plate, place the warm octopus on top and sprinkle over the red onion, dill and cumin. Drizzle over the final tablespoon of olive oil and serve with the olives and lemon wedges.

CUTTLEFISH, CHICKPEAS AND CHILLI OIL

Sometimes it is better to treat large squid like cuttlefish and simmer it gently for 30-40 minutes, so it melts in the mouth. An advantage of slow cooking is that sumptuous juices are released to help produce the sauce.

Serves 4

CHILLI OIL

6 large red chillies, seeds left in, finely chopped

12 tablespoons extra virgin olive oil

CUTTLEFISH AND CHICKPEAS

400g cuttlefish or large squid

½ large carrot, finely chopped

1 red onion, finely chopped

2 medium tomatoes, finely chopped

100ml fino sherry or white wine

1 celery stick, finely chopped (optional)

400g can of chickpeas, undrained

2 teaspoons finely chopped rosemary

2 bay leaves, preferably fresh

1 tablespoon chopped flat-leaf parsley

3 tablespoons olive oil

2 garlic cloves, finely chopped

To make the chilli oil, season the chopped chillies with salt, transfer to a sterilised Kilner jar and mix with the olive oil. It can be eaten immediately or left for 2-3 weeks in the fridge for the flavour and colour to develop.

Now for the cuttlefish. Start by holding the cuttlefish over a sink with the bony cuttle touching your palm. Using a small knife, make a small incision in the cavity that houses the guts (opposite the cuttle). Gently remove and discard all these bits including the grey ink sac. Turn the cuttlefish in your palm so the cuttle is now on top and pull it out. If this proves difficult, make another incision along the side and it should slip out. Peel off as much of the skin as possible. Pull out the black beaky mouth at the centre of the tentacles. Wash the cuttlefish under running water.

Place all the ingredients apart from the olive oil and garlic in a large saucepan and bring to a gentle simmer, with the lid on. Meanwhile, in a small pan, heat the olive oil over a medium heat and fry the garlic until nutty brown. Pour the garlic and oil over the cuttlefish and simmer for 30-45 minutes. The only way to know if the cuttlefish or squid is tender is to have a nibble or prod a thick piece with a blunt knife to see if it goes through with ease. When it is ready, lift the cuttlefish or squid out on to a board, divide any tentacles into pieces and slice the body into 1cm x 2.5cm strips. Stir them back into the chickpea mixture, return to a simmer and taste for seasoning. To serve, tranfer to a dish and spoon over some chilli oil.

BLACK RICE, CUTTLEFISH AND PRESERVED LEMON

Every Spanish cookery book has a recipe for this, and jolly good they are too, but thanks to the chef Natalie Smith, we now always use preserved lemon in this dish. It is a wonderful improvement and we have never looked back. Hooray for the original mind! Both squid ink and preserved lemons can be quite salty, so check for seasoning only after you have added both of these.

Serves 4-6

CUTTLEFISH OR SQUID
500-600g cuttlefish or large squid, prepared and cleaned (page 198)
2 fresh bay leaves
1 sprig of rosemary
1 sprig of thyme
1 tablespoon olive oil
2 tablespoons white wine

BLACK RICE
8 tablespoons olive oil
2 Romano peppers (page 280), finely diced
1 green pepper, finely diced
1 large onion, finely chopped

4 fresh bay leaves
2 teaspoons thyme leaves
1 tablespoon finely chopped rosemary
½ teaspoon smoked sweet Spanish paprika (page 280)
200g paella rice
1 tablespoon finely chopped preserved lemon rind (page 280)
2 x 4g sachets squid ink (page 281)
a squeeze of lemon
1 tablespoon shredded flat-leaf parsley
1 quantity of Alioli (page 161) (optional)

Place the cuttlefish or squid in a large pot with the herbs, olive oil and wine. Cover with water by 5cm and simmer for 35-45 minutes, or until tender. To check if it's ready, insert a small skewer through the thickest part of a tentacle. When it goes through without rubbery resistance, it's done. Remove the cuttlefish or squid, reserving 800ml of the cooking liquor, and when cool enough, slice into 1cm x 2cm pieces.

To make the rice base, heat the oil in a heavy-based pan and add the peppers, onion, bay leaves, thyme, rosemary, paprika and a small pinch of salt. Cook over a medium heat for 15-20 minutes, stirring occasionally, until the vegetables are soft and beginning to caramelise. Add the rice and half the preserved lemon and stir over a low heat for a few minutes. Add the sachets of squid ink to the reserved cuttlefish liquor, mix well and add to the rice pan with the cuttlefish. Give the ingredients a good stir, cover with a lid and simmer gently, without stirring, for 15-20 minutes, until the rice is fractionally al dente. The rice will continue to cook off the heat, so it is important to remove it just before it is ready. Let it rest for 5 minutes. Stir in the remaining preserved lemon, a squeeze of lemon juice and scatter over the parsley. At Morito we serve this rice with a spoonful or two of alioli.

EX❤
MARKET

MUSHROOM AND PRAWN RICE

Over the years, our tastes have leant towards wetter, almost soupy styles of rice. If you prefer it drier, simply reduce the amount of stock; you can always add more if necessary. This is served as an early-autumn rice tapa at Morito, when the chanterelle mushrooms start to arrive from Scotland.

Serves 4-6

400g raw or cooked North Atlantic prawns (page 281), shell-on, peeled and shells reserved

1 celery stick, roughly chopped

1 carrot, roughly chopped

1 white onion, roughly chopped

a few parsley stalks

a few black peppercorns

a generous splash of fino sherry or white wine

10 tablespoons olive oil

400g chanterelle or oyster mushrooms, cleaned and halved

1 large Spanish onion, finely chopped

1 garlic clove, finely chopped

1 fennel bulb, finely chopped

3 spring onions, finely chopped

4 bay leaves, preferably fresh

500g cherry tomatoes, blitzed

200g paella rice

2 tablespoons shredded flat-leaf parsley

1 quantity of Alioli (page 161)

lemon wedges, to serve

Put the prawn shells into a large saucepan with the celery, carrot, onion, parsley stalks, black peppercorns and sherry or wine. Just cover with water and simmer for 10-15 minutes, then remove from the heat and set aside. Strain the stock and measure out 800ml.

Heat 3 tablespoons of the olive oil in a large, heavy-based pan over a medium-high heat. Add the mushrooms and a pinch of salt and fry for 3-5 minutes, stirring occasionally, until soft and beginning to caramelise. Remove the mushrooms with a slotted spoon and set aside. Now add the remaining oil to the pan along with the onion, garlic, fennel, spring onions and bay leaves. Season and cook for 10 minutes, stirring occasionally, until soft and beginning to caramelise. Stir in the blitzed tomatoes and cook for another 10-15 minutes, then add the rice and stir for a minute or two to coat. Meanwhile reheat the reserved stock and pour it over the rice, give everything a good stir and cover with a lid. Cook gently over a low heat, without stirring, for 15-20 minutes until the rice is just al dente.

Add the prawns and mushrooms to the pan and cook for 2-3 minutes if using raw prawns, 1 minute if using cooked ones. Remove from the heat, check the seasoning and let the rice rest for 5 minutes. It will continue to cook a little after it has been taken off the heat. Transfer to a plate, sprinkle with the parsley and serve with the alioli and lemon wedges.

FIDEOS WITH CLAMS

Another great sharing dish.

Serves 4

9 tablespoons olive oil

1 small onion, finely chopped

1 leek, halved lengthways and finely sliced

1 green pepper, finely chopped

10 cherry tomatoes, chopped

1 red chilli, deseeded and finely chopped

3 sprigs of lemon thyme or ordinary thyme

zest of 1 lemon

4 bay leaves, preferably fresh

½ teaspoon fennel seeds, crushed

160g fideos (page 281) or angel hair pasta broken into
  2cm pieces

25 surf clams, cockles or mussels, cleaned and rinsed

1 tablespoon shredded flat-leaf parsley

a sprinkling of smoked Spanish paprika (page 280)

1 quantity of Alioli (page 161)

½ lemon, cut into wedges

SHELLFISH STOCK

1 leek, roughly chopped

2 carrots, roughly chopped

1 onion, roughly sliced

4 bay leaves, preferably fresh

1 teaspoon fennel seeds

1 teaspoon black peppercorns

1 sprig of lemon thyme or ordinary thyme

500g prawn shells, crab and/or langoustine shells

200ml white wine

60ml brandy

20 threads of saffron, steeped in 100ml boiling water

For the stock, place the leek, carrots, onion, bay leaves, fennel seeds, peppercorns and thyme in a large saucepan, just cover with water and simmer for 15 minutes. Add the crustacean shells and simmer for another 15 minutes. Remove from the heat, strain the liquid and discard the solids. Add the wine, brandy and saffron-infused water to the strained liquid, return to a medium heat and simmer for 10 minutes. Season with salt and pepper to taste.

Heat 6 tablespoons of the olive oil in a wide pan, stir in the onion, leek, green pepper, tomatoes, chilli, thyme, lemon zest, bay leaves and fennel seeds. Season with salt and cook gently over a medium heat for 15-20 minutes, stirring occasionally, until soft and beginning to caramelise.

Remove from the heat and set aside.

Preheat the oven to 200°C/400°F/Gas 6. Over a medium heat, heat the remaining 3 tablespoons of olive oil in a paella pan or ovenproof frying pan (about 25cm in diameter). Add the fideos and fry for a few minutes until they begin to brown. Remove from the heat, then stir in the vegetable mixture and just enough shellfish stock to cover – around 500ml. Mix everything together gently, check the seasoning and place the clams on top. Bring to a gentle simmer over a medium heat, then place in the hot oven for 10-15 minutes, or until the clams have opened and most of the stock has been absorbed. Remove from the oven, check the seasoning once more and sprinkle with the parsley and paprika. Serve with lemon wedges and alioli.

MUSSEL AND CHORIZO EMPANADILLAS

Makes 8 empanadillas

PASTRY

- 25g butter
- 50ml whole milk
- 1½ tablespoons olive oil
- 200g plain flour, plus extra for dusting
- 125g polenta (page 281)
- 100ml white wine

EMPANADILLA FILLING

- 1kg mussels, cleaned, debearded and rinsed
- 4 tablespoons olive oil
- 80g cooking chorizo, chopped (page 281)
- 1 onion, finely chopped
- 1 small red pepper, finely chopped
- 1 small green pepper, finely chopped
- 4 fresh bay leaves
- 1 garlic clove, finely chopped
- ½ teaspoon fennel seeds, ground
- ½ teaspoon smoked hot Spanish paprika (page 280) or chilli
- 200g cherry tomatoes, blitzed
- a splash of white wine
- 1½ tablespoons finely chopped flat-leaf parsley

TO FRY THE EMPANADILLA

- 300ml sunflower, olive or rapeseed oil

To make the pastry, put the butter, milk and oil in a small saucepan and heat gently until the butter has melted. Place the flour, polenta and a good pinch of salt in a large bowl. Add the warm liquid to the bowl, together with the wine, and knead to form a soft dough. Wrap the dough in cling film, flatten it and let it rest in the fridge for 20 minutes.

For the filling, place the mussels in a large pan over a high heat, lid on, until just opened. Drain in a colander and, when cool enough, remove the mussels from their shells. Discard any that have not opened.

Heat a frying pan over a high heat, add 1 tablespoon of the olive oil and fry the chorizo for 2 minutes. Remove from the pan and set aside. Heat the remaining olive oil in the pan, still over a high heat, and stir in the chopped vegetables with the bay leaves, garlic, fennel and paprika or chilli. Cook for 10 minutes until soft, then add the tomatoes and wine. Cook for another 10 minutes, return the chorizo to the pan with the mussels and parsley, mix well and remove from the heat. Check the seasoning.

Lightly flour a large work surface and roll out the dough to 3–4mm thick. Use a saucer to cut it into discs, around 10cm in diameter. Fill one half of each disc with the mussel mixture, fold to create a half-moon-shaped parcel and seal by pressing the edges together with a fork. Trim off any excess pastry (the frilly edge should be about 1cm wide). Heat the oil in a deep frying pan, add the empanadillas in batches and fry over a medium-high heat for a few minutes, until golden brown on both sides. Eat immediately.

MUSSELS, FETA AND DILL

The different textures of the mussels and fennel are excellent together, and the fragrant tomato and feta sauce makes this dish special.

Serves 4
4 tablespoons olive oil, plus extra to serve
1 onion, finely chopped
1 fennel bulb, chopped
1 green pepper, chopped
2 garlic cloves, chopped
2 bay leaves, preferably fresh
200g cherry tomatoes, blitzed
a pinch of sugar (optional)
3 tablespoons white wine
1kg mussels, cleaned, debearded and rinsed
150g feta cheese, crumbled
1-2 teaspoons deseeded and finely chopped red chilli
1 tablespoon shredded flat-leaf parsley
1 tablespoon roughly chopped dill

Heat a wide saucepan over a high heat, then add the olive oil, followed shortly by the onion, fennel, green pepper, garlic, bay leaves and some salt and pepper. Fry for 5-10 minutes until soft, stirring occasionally, then add the tomatoes, plus the optional sugar if the tomatoes aren't very sweet, and the wine. Cook for another 5 minutes.

Add the mussels, cover the pan and let them steam, still over a high heat, until they open. Remove from the heat, discard any that are not open, then stir in the feta, chilli, parsley and dill, and check the seasoning. Finish with a drizzle of olive oil and serve immediately, with bread.

MUSSELS, PRAWNS AND CHORIZO

Prawns are optional in this recipe.

Serves 4
600g cherry tomatoes
4 tablespoons olive oil
180g hot cooking chorizo (page 281), finely chopped
1 garlic clove, finely chopped
1kg mussels, cleaned, debearded and rinsed
400g tin or jar cooked chickpeas (page 281), drained
50ml fino sherry
pinch of sugar
100g raw or cooked peeled North Atlantic prawns (page 281)
   (optional)
1 tablespoon shredded flat-leaf parsley
1-2 teaspoons fresh chopped red chilli, Chilli Oil (page 198)
   or Harissa (page 176) (optional)

Bring a small pot of water to the boil and blanch the cherry tomatoes in it for 20 seconds. Drain and cool under running water. Peel the tomatoes and chop roughly. Heat the olive oil in a large saucepan over a high heat. Add the chorizo and cook for a few minutes, until it begins to crisp slightly at the edges. Add the garlic and cook for another minute. Now add the tomatoes, mussels, chickpeas, sherry, sugar and a pinch of salt and continue to cook for a few minutes, lid on, until the mussels open. If the prawns are raw, add them just as the mussels begin to open; if cooked, stir in 1 minute before serving, just to heat through.

Remove from the heat and transfer the mixture to a bowl. Check the seasoning, sprinkle with the parsley and serve immediately, with the chilli or harissa.

SEA BASS ROE A LA PLANCHA

Available from late spring to early summer, fresh sea bass roe is a delicate and special thing. Ask your fishmonger to save some for you. Delicious with raw fennel salad and alioli.

> **Serves 4**
> **400g sea bass roe**
> **Maldon salt**
> **3 tablespoons good-quality extra virgin olive oil**
> **juice and zest of 1 lemon**
> **1 tablespoon finely chopped flat-leaf parsley**
> **1 quantity of Alioli (page 161)**

Season the roe well with salt and set aside for 10 minutes. Heat a heavy-based frying pan or plancha pan over a high heat. Pat the roe dry with kitchen paper and then rub all over with a small amount of the olive oil. Place in the hot pan, cook until golden brown underneath, then turn them over and colour the other side. At Morito we half cook them, so they are a little bit rare (and soft) in the middle, which benefits their texture.

Put the roe on a chopping board and carefully slice into 1.5cm discs with a sharp knife. Place on a warm plate and drizzle over the remaining olive oil. Sprinkle over the lemon juice and zest, parsley and some salt and serve with the alioli.

FISH HEAD, DATES AND SHERRY VINEGAR

Fish are precious and fish are rare, so when we receive a large sea bass, halibut or turbot from the coast, we never throw the head away. We have learnt over the years that it is a thing to be prized. Mostly the cheeks are the real delicacy, yet there are surprisingly delicious pickings to be had all over. Ask your fishmonger to put some heads aside for you. We deep-fry the heads because it is quick and you achieve a little bit of crunch on the skin. The alternative is to omit the flour and bake the heads, covered with foil.

Serves 2–4
2 large fish heads, well scaled
6 small or 3 large dates or 3 tablespoons date molasses
** (page 280)**
3 tablespoons sherry vinegar (page 280)
½ teaspoon ground coriander
2 tablespoons extra virgin olive oil
⅓ garlic clove, crushed with a little salt
¾ teaspoon deseeded and finely chopped green chilli
1 tablespoon chopped coriander
a pinch of brown sugar (optional)
2–3 tablespoons plain flour
500–700ml sunflower oil or rapeseed oil, for deep-frying
rocket and lemon wedges, to serve

Season the heads all over with salt, rubbing it in slightly. Allow the salt to penetrate for at least 10 minutes. Stone the dates and chop them very finely. Place the vinegar, dates or date molasses, ground coriander and olive oil in a small saucepan and simmer over a medium heat for 3 minutes, until reduced. Stir and break up the dates as they cook, to give a smooth sauce and to prevent sticking. Add the garlic, chilli and chopped coriander to the pan with a splash or two of water to give a light, saucy consistency. Taste and season with salt, brown sugar and a good pinch of black pepper, then pour into a small serving bowl or ramekin.

Coat the fish heads thickly with the flour. In a saucepan large enough to fry one head at a time, heat up enough oil over a medium-high heat to cover. Carefully lower a fish head into the oil and fry until it is a dark golden colour. Remove and place on kitchen paper to drain. Fry the second head in the same manner. We recommend eating this dish with your fingers and spooning on bits of sauce as you go.

MEAT

SPICED LAMB, AUBERGINE AND MINT

We found this Turkish recipe while watching videos on YouTube. It is an excellent way of learning about real, home-cooked food, and as it is a visual medium it doesn't matter about the language barrier.

Serves 4

SPICED LAMB

- 600g lamb shank, off the bone
- 1 teaspoon coriander seeds
- 1 teaspoon cumin seeds
- 1 cinnamon stick
- 1 onion, halved
- 2 sprigs of thyme
- 3 bay leaves, preferably fresh

AUBERGINE

- 4 aubergines
- 4 tablespoons strained Greek yoghurt, such as Total
- 4 tablespoons extra virgin olive oil
- 1 small garlic clove, crushed to a paste with ½ teaspoon salt
- juice of ½ lemon

TO CRISP THE LAMB

- 50g butter
- 1 large Spanish onion, thinly sliced
- ½ teaspoon cumin seeds, lightly toasted and ground (page 34)
- 1 teaspoon ground cinnamon

TO SERVE

- 1 quantity of Chilli Butter (page 116)
- 1 tablespoon shredded mint
- 1 tablespoon pine nuts, toasted
- 2 tablespoons pomegranate seeds

Put the lamb, coriander, cumin, cinnamon, onion, thyme, bay leaves and ½ teaspoon of salt in a saucepan and cover with water. Simmer for 30-40 minutes, skimming off any froth that builds up, until the meat is tender and falls apart when handled. Remove the lamb from the pot. When cool enough to handle, shred the meat, discarding any small bones or fat.

Grill the aubergines, ideally whole over a barbecue for a smoky flavour (page 144), or bake for about 45 minutes in a hot oven (240°C/475°F/Gas 9) until soft. Remove and leave to cool. Peel the aubergines and place the flesh in a bowl. Add the yoghurt, olive oil, garlic and lemon juice. Season with salt and pepper and mix well.

To crisp the lamb, melt the butter in a saucepan, add the onion with a pinch of salt and cook slowly for 10-15 minutes, until soft, golden and sweet. Add the cumin and cinnamon, fry for 1 minute, then add the lamb and continue to cook, stirring occasionally, until the lamb is part crispy and part still moist and juicy. Check the seasoning.

To serve, spread the aubergine purée on a plate and sprinkle the hot, crispy lamb on top, followed by the warm chilli butter, mint, pine nuts and pomegranate seeds.

LAMB CHOPS MECHOUI

A Morito favourite, this is delicious with Flatbread, Chopped Salad and
Spiced Labneh (pages 10, 108 and 91)

Serves 4
12-16 lamb chops, depending on their size

MARINADE
2 garlic cloves, crushed to a paste with ½ teaspoon salt
¼ onion, finely grated
1 teaspoon smoked Spanish paprika, hot or sweet (page 280)
2 teaspoons freshly ground cumin seeds
2 tablespoons olive oil
2 tablespoons lemon juice

TO COOK THE LAMB
2 tablespoons cumin seeds, freshly ground
½ teaspoon sweet paprika (page 280)
½ teaspoon hot paprika (page 280)
1 teaspoon Maldon salt
1 lemon, cut into quarters

Mix the garlic, onion, spices, oil and lemon juice together thoroughly in a
bowl, then add the lamb chops and turn to coat them really well. Cover and
leave for an hour at room temperature or overnight in the fridge.

When you are ready to cook the lamb, mix the cumin, paprikas and salt
together in a bowl. Sprinkle the lamb liberally with half the spice mixture.
Place the chops under a hot grill, on a barbecue or smoking-hot griddle pan
and cook for 5-8 minutes on either side for pink, turning once or twice.
Serve immediately, with the remaining cumin mixture and the lemon on the side.

LAMB KEBABS

On Exmouth Market, the street where Morito and Moro live, we also have a food stall. We feed the creative and mostly merry workers of the area every weekday for the princely sum of £5. For the lamb kebabs we use Spiced Lamb (page 218) or marinated leg or fillet that is barbecued or flash-fried.

Serves 4

MARINATED LAMB

- 1 quantity of Spiced Lamb (page 218) or 240g trimmed lamb leg or fillet
- 1 garlic clove, crushed to a paste with ½ teaspoon salt
- ⅓ teaspoon smoked Spanish paprika, hot or sweet (page 280)
- ½ teaspoon freshly ground cumin seeds
- ¼ teaspoon ground cinnamon
- 1 tablespoon olive oil
- 1 tablespoon lemon juice

If using leg or fillet, cut the lamb into 1cm-thick slices, then into bite-sized squares, either to go on a skewer or to flash-fry. Mix all the remaining ingredients together in a bowl, then add the lamb and turn to coat really well. Cover the lamb and leave for an hour at room temperature or overnight in the fridge.

If you are barbecuing the lamb, thread the pieces on to 4 small skewers through the thin edge of the meat (so each skewer is 1cm thick). As soon as the flames have died down from the charcoal, put the skewers on the grill, season with salt and cook for 2 minutes on each side, until the lamb is slightly charred on the outside and pink in the middle. Remove and keep warm.

If you are flash-frying the lamb, wait until you are ready to assemble (i.e. the salad is dressed and the flatbread is warm), then place a large frying pan or wok over a high heat. When it is hot, add the meat, season and cook, stirring continuously, for 1 minute. Turn off the heat and keep warm.

TO ASSEMBLE THE KEBAB

BREAD

The flatbread you use really depends on the time you have and what you can lay your hands on. There is Morito Flatbread, of course (page 10), but otherwise any authentic fresh pitta or pocket bread will do. Briefly warming the bread always brings it alive. We allow half a bread per person.

SALAD

Thickly sliced romaine or cos lettuce hearts, a few rocket leaves and a little finely shredded white cabbage, a little chopped tomato, chopped mint, flat-leaf parsley and coriander and some chopped deseeded red chillies all simply dressed with olive oil and lemon juice.

EXTRAS

At the market stall we always serve the lamb flatbreads with Hummus (page 107). If using bought hummus, add a little extra lemon juice and olive oil to jazz it up. We spread roughly 1 tablespoon of hummus on each warm flatbread before assembling with the chopped salad, sliced Turkish pickled chillies (page 280), some seasoned yoghurt, chilli flakes (page 280) and the hot lamb.

GAZIANTEP KIBBEH

Gaziantep is an ancient and charming city in south-east Turkey that grows the best pistachios in the world. This kibbeh recipe is not technically very hard and doesn't take a crazy amount of time. What revolutionised the speed and quality of our kibbeh-making was a Gaziantep chef, Fatte, who showed us how you first freeze the centres before covering them with the thin outer casing. They are something special, so do please give them a go.

If accompanied by other mezzes such as Chopped Salad (page 108) then these kibbeh won't need anything else other than some garlicky yoghurt or Labneh (page 91).

Makes 8 kibbeh
600g trimmed lamb shoulder, finely minced
2 tablespoons olive oil
25g butter
1 large red onion, chopped
3 garlic cloves, chopped
2 teaspoons freshly ground cumin seeds
1 teaspoon ground cinnamon
¾ teaspoon Aleppo chilli flakes (page 280) or ½ teaspoon
   cayenne pepper or chilli powder
100g unsalted pistachios, roughly chopped
2 tablespoons chopped flat-leaf parsley
2 tablespoons pomegranate molasses (page 280)
100g medium bulgur
800ml sunflower oil, for deepish frying

Divide the minced lamb into 2 parts: 250g for the stuffing and 350g for the casing.

For the stuffing, warm the olive oil and butter in a frying pan over a medium heat and cook the onion for about 10 minutes, stirring occasionally, until softened. Add the garlic, 1½ teaspoons of the cumin and half the cinnamon. Fry for a couple of minutes then add the 250g of lamb and the chilli. It is important when the lamb is cooking initially that you stir it well into the onion and spices to stop large lumps forming. Fry for 3-4 minutes, until you start to get some caramelisation on the meat. Season with salt and pepper, then add the pistachios, parsley and pomegranate molasses. Stir everything well, then remove from the heat and leave to cool. To speed up the cooling process, spread the mix out on a baking tray or plate and put it in the fridge for 20 minutes.

When the mixture is cold, divide it into 8 equal piles and squeeze each pile quite hard in the hand to make a small oval shape that holds together. Leave these in the freezer for 1 hour or cover and freeze for up to 2 weeks.

To make the casing, place the bulgur in a large bowl and add enough hot water from the tap to cover it by 3-4mm. Stir in a pinch of salt and leave the bulgur to suck up the water for 10 minutes. Meanwhile, place the remaining 350g of lamb in a food processor with a pinch of salt and the rest of the cumin and cinnamon. Pulse briefly to make it a little bit smoother and stickier. When the bulgur is dry, add the lamb and knead well together by hand or with a wooden spoon. Divide the mix into 8 equal portions.

Remove the frozen centres from the freezer one at a time. Flatten a portion of the outer mix on the palm of your hand. Nestle the frozen stuffing in the centre and surround it with the casing as thinly as possible with no cracks. At this point the actual shaping is purely aesthetic and, although never our strong point, it is worth spending a little time trying to create a cute lemon shape, otherwise the browned result can be slightly off-putting.

Coat and shape the rest of the kibbeh and refrigerate until you are ready to fry. (At this point they will keep for 1-2 days or can be frozen.)

When you are ready to eat, pour the oil into a deep-fat fryer or large saucepan, making sure it comes no more than halfway up the side of the pan. Heat to about 180°C/350°F. Fry the kibbeh until dark brown. If frying from frozen, probe the centre with a sharp knife to check if it is hot all the way through. Serve immediately.

MORITO MERGUEZ

You will need a mincer and a sausage-making attachment on your food processor
– or ask your friendly butcher for help!

Makes 20 merguez
750g boned lamb shoulder, trimmed
250g beef fat
2 teaspoons fine salt
1 small onion, grated
3 garlic cloves, crushed
2 red chillies, deseeded and finely chopped
1 small bunch of coriander, chopped
75g Rich Tea biscuits, crushed into fine crumbs
½ teaspoon fennel seeds, roughly ground
1 heaped teaspoon hot paprika (page 280)
1 heaped teaspoon sweet paprika (page 280)
1 heaped teaspoon ground cinnamon
1 heaped teaspoon freshly ground black pepper
1 heaped teaspoon coriander seeds, roughly ground
1 heaped teaspoon cumin seeds, roughly ground
1½ teaspoons caraway seeds, roughly ground
natural chipolata skins (page 281)

Pass the lamb once through the coarse plate and once through the fine plate
of your mincer. If your sausage stuffer minces the mixture as it goes into
the casings, then mince your lamb only once. Now separately mince the
beef fat through the fine plate. Mix the salt with the grated onion, adding
a tablespoon of water to help the salt dissolve. Mix and knead all the
remaining stuffing ingredients together until everything is well incorporated.
Now the fun begins!

Unravel the skins on to your sausage-making attachment. Place the
sausage meat in the machine ready to go. Really at this point, we believe
that sausage making is a two-person job. One person gently coaxes the meat
into the machine and is in charge of the on/off switch; the other controls
the mixture filling the skins. Do not fill the merguez too tightly, as they
tighten up quite a bit when you twist them. All of this takes a little bit
of practice and causes a great deal of giggling. Sausage skins are cheap, so
have another go if you are not happy with your results.

When you have used up all the meat, pinch the sausage into 15cm lengths
and twist. Leave in the fridge overnight to mature. They will keep, if
refrigerated, for up to 5 days or can be frozen. Fry or grill until just
cooked, then serve either in a bread roll with Harissa (page 176) or simply
with a little salad.

LAMB AND PRUNE TAGINE

This warming tagine is a Moroccan classic. Sweet, savoury and spicy, it is perfect for autumnal and wintry days.

Serves 4
1 tablespoon olive oil
30g butter
250g onions, grated
1½ teaspoons ground ginger
2½ teaspoons ground cinnamon
1 bunch of coriander, roughly chopped, plus extra to garnish
500g boneless lamb shank, trimmed and cut into 3-4cm chunks
15 threads of saffron, steeped in 3 tablespoons boiling water
300g pitted prunes, soaked in hot water until soft, drained
1 tablespoon honey

Heat the oil and butter in a saucepan over a medium heat. When the butter starts to foam, add the onions, ginger, cinnamon, coriander and a pinch of salt and cook for 5-10 minutes, until the onions become soft and light brown. Add the meat and stir for a few minutes, until it begins to brown and is nicely coated with the spices. Add enough water to cover the meat by about 4cm, then add the saffron-infused water and bring to the boil. Lower the heat, add half of the prunes and simmer for about 45 minutes until the meat starts to soften.

Add the remaining prunes and the honey and continue cooking for 20-30 minutes or until the meat is very tender and almost melting. Check for seasoning then sprinkle with more coriander and serve with couscous or bread.

PASTIRMA

Pastirma is the Turkish version of that New York Jewish deli classic,
pastrami. We had often read about this in cookbooks, yet were put off by
the overprocessed samples available to buy. Inevitably in this situation, we
resort to making our own. Traditionally beef brisket is used for pastirma.
Sometimes we use what is known as the salmon cut, which lives next door
to the brisket and happens to be the piece that is used for the Italian
bresaola. We generally brine our pastirma for 12 days. Even if you have a
piece of beef weighing quite a bit more than 600g, it will still only need
12 days as long as it is around 10cm thick.

Once the meat has been cured and then marinated, we hang it next door
at Moro, just to one side of the charcoal grill where it is not too hot,
so the meat won't cook, yet it dries well and attracts a little bit of the
smoke. For drying at home, it is a bit of a tricky one, because the smell of
the marinade is pungent and you will have to accept that it will be noticed
in whichever room it is hanging. With this in mind, we would probably hang it
near the extraction over the cooker, or as much out of the way as possible.

Serves 10-12
600g piece of beef, trimmed of sinew and fat

BRINE SOLUTION
4 litres water
250g salt
4 handfuls of sugar
1 level tablespoon ground fenugreek seeds
1 level tablespoon crushed dried red chillies
1 tablespoon coriander seeds, crushed or ground

MARINADE
1 medium onion, finely grated
2 teaspoons ground fenugreek seeds
2 teaspoons Aleppo chilli flakes (page 280) or hot paprika
(page 280)
3 teaspoons ground coriander seeds
1 teaspoon freshly ground black pepper

First you will need to find a stainless-steel, plastic or non-reactive
container or a saucepan with a lid large enough to hold the brine solution
and the beef but small enough to fit in the fridge.

Mix all the brine ingredients together in your chosen container until
most of the salt has dissolved. Pop the beef into the brine and place a small
plate over it to keep it submerged, then cover with a lid or some cling film.
Leave in the fridge to cure for 12 days.

After the 12 days are up, drain the beef and pat it dry with kitchen paper. Mix all the marinade ingredients together in a bowl and allow them to sit for 15 minutes so the spices swell. Coat the beef well with the mix – don't be alarmed by the slimy texture the fenugreek gives it. With a clean sterilised butcher's hook, hang up the beef in its desired location. In the hot, smoky kitchen at Moro, the drying process takes only 3 days, but at home it will take 1-2 weeks. The pastirma should feel firm and rubbery, not spongy. Do not fret too much about how long to hang it for, as mostly it is down to personal taste how soft or dense the end result is.

Serving and storage suggestions
We usually serve pastirma, sliced as thinly as possible, either with a tomato salad, an orange and potato salad or Beetroot, Almonds and Mint (page 97), or warm pitta, stuffed with hummus, watercress and sliced pickles. Store pastirma in the fridge, wrapped in greaseproof paper, for up to a month.

CHICHARRONES DE CÁDIZ

Chicharrones are a meatier and classier variation of pork scratchings. This Cádiz version is made by slow-roasting belly of pork, chopping it up and serving it with lots of freshly squeezed lemon juice and ground cumin.

Serves 4-6

2 garlic cloves, crushed to a paste with 1 teaspoon salt

1 tablespoon ground fennel seeds

1kg piece of organic or free-range pork belly, skin scored

2 teaspoons fine sea salt

½ medium onion, peeled

½ lemon, cut into wedges, to serve (optional)

TO FINISH

juice of 2 lemons

3 teaspoons cumin seeds, lightly toasted and roughly ground (page 34)

The following is the Moro recipe for roast pork belly, but if you have a tried and trusted method, feel free to use your own.

Preheat the oven to 230°C/450°F/Gas 8. Mix the garlic with the fennel seeds and rub it over the flesh side of the pork belly. Turn the meat over and dry the skin thoroughly – a hair dryer works well. Generously sprinkle the skin with the salt. Leave for 20 minutes, then dust off the excess salt.

Place the onion half in a roasting tin and put the pork belly on top to create a convex shape, which will help the crackling form. Place on the top shelf of the oven. It is important that the oven is really hot to start with, in order to blister the skin and create good crackling. Roast at this high heat for 20-30 minutes or until hard crackling has formed, then reduce the heat to 190°C/375°F/Gas 5. Pour 3 tablespoons of water into the bottom of the pan to prevent the meat juices burning. Continue to cook for about 2 hours or until the meat is soft and tender. Cool completely and remove any bones. Dice the pork into generous bite-sized cubes.

Heat a frying pan until hot, but don't add any oil. Fry the cubes of pork until they have caramelised, crisped up and heated through. Transfer to a plate, squeeze over plenty of lemon juice and sprinkle liberally with the cumin. Add extra salt to taste if needed.

SWEET-SOUR PX PORK

The initial slow-roasting of the pork can be done a day or two in advance.
PX stands for Pedro Ximénez, the sweet, raisiny sherry from Jerez.

Serves 4-6
3 garlic cloves, crushed to a paste with 1 teaspoon salt
1½ teaspoons finely chopped rosemary
1kg piece of organic or free-range pork belly, skin scored
2 teaspoons fine sea salt
½ medium onion, peeled
50ml sherry vinegar (page 280)
120ml Pedro Ximénez sherry
3 bay leaves, preferably fresh

Preheat the oven to 230°C/450°F/Gas 8. Mix the garlic with the rosemary and
smear it over the flesh side of the pork belly. Turn the meat over and dry the
skin thoroughly - a hair dryer works well. Generously sprinkle the skin with
the salt. Leave for 20 minutes, then dust off the excess salt.

Place the onion half in a roasting tin and put the pork belly on top
to create a convex shape, which will help the crackling form. Place on the
top shelf of the oven. It is important that the oven is really hot to start
with, to blister the skin and create good crackling. Roast at this high heat
for 20-30 minutes or until hard crackling has formed, then reduce the heat to
190°C/375°F/Gas 5. Pour 3 tablespoons of water into the bottom of the pan, to
prevent the meat juices burning. Continue to cook for about 2 hours or until
the meat is soft and tender. Remove from the oven and cool for half an hour.
Place the pork belly on a chopping board. Remove the crackling and discard
any exposed fat if you wish. With a strong knife, cut the crackling and the
pork into bite-sized pieces, removing any bones.

Discard two-thirds of the hot fat that has come off the pork in the
roasting tin. Pour in the vinegar and sherry to loosen any caramelised juices
over a low heat, if necessary. Blitz these juices with the roasted onion,
using a hand-held blender or food processor, then return the sauce to the
pan, adding a pinch of black pepper and the bay leaves. Check for seasoning.

Turn the oven up to 220°C/425°F/Gas 7. Transfer the pork (not the
crackling) to the roasting pan and coat well in the sauce. Cook the pork for
20-30 minutes, until the sauce is thick and rich, basting and turning the
meat halfway through cooking. Serve immediately, with the warm crackling
scattered on top.

BUTIFARRA, WHITE BEANS AND ALIOLI

Butifarra is the Catalan word for sausage. There are many different shapes, sizes and styles. What sets them apart from chorizo is not just that they are from Catalunya but that they are rarely red with paprika. If you are ever in Barcelona, there is a great shop called La Botifarreria opposite Santa Maria church, east of Las Ramblas. You can adapt this recipe to use with your favourite sausages, though when you eat the familiar sausages with white beans and alioli they will no longer taste quite so familiar.

Serves 4-6

150g dried white cannellini beans, soaked in cold water overnight (or 2 x 400g tins of white beans)

2 bay leaves, preferably fresh (if using dried beans)

6-7 tablespoons extra virgin olive oil

1 onion, halved (if using dried beans)

2-3 garlic cloves, finely chopped

2 tablespoons finely chopped flat-leaf parsley

3 butifarra sausages (about 200g) (page 281), sliced into 1.5cm-thick discs

1 quantity of Alioli (page 161)

Drain the soaked beans, place in a saucepan and add enough fresh water to cover by 5cm. Add the bay leaves, 1 tablespoon of the olive oil and the onion and simmer over a medium heat for around 45 minutes to 1 hour. Check the beans after 40 minutes, as pulses vary in cooking time depending on their quality and age. Ideally they should be really soft and almost falling apart. When they are ready, remove from the heat, drain off any excess cooking liquor until level with the beans and season with salt and pepper. If using tinned beans, drain off a little of the liquid and heat the beans in a pan.

Heat 5 tablespoons of olive oil in a pan, add the chopped garlic and fry until golden. Stir in 1½ tablespoons of the parsley, fry for a few more seconds and then add to the beans. Stir well, so that all the flavours merge, returning the pan to the heat if the beans need to be reheated.

Place another frying pan over a high heat and fry the butifarra in the remaining tablespoon of olive oil until crisp on both sides. Check the beans for seasoning, then spoon them into a bowl and place the sausage on top. Sprinkle with the remaining parsley and serve with the alioli.

JAMÓN CROQUETAS

The mark of a good jamón croqueta is a velvety smooth béchamel.

Makes about 15 croquetas
100g butter
1 small onion, very finely chopped
100g chicken breast, very finely chopped
150g jamón (page 281), very finely chopped
½ nutmeg, grated
150g plain flour, sifted
1.25 litres chicken stock, lightly seasoned
1 handful of shredded flat-leaf parsley
1 litre vegetable oil, for deep-frying
2 organic or free-range eggs, lightly beaten
150g breadcrumbs

Melt the butter in a heavy-based pan, add the onion and cook over a medium heat for 10 minutes, until soft and translucent. Add the chicken breast and cook for another 5 minutes. Stir in the jamón, nutmeg and flour and reduce the heat to low. Cook slowly, stirring often with a wooden spoon, to prevent the flour burning. After a few minutes the flour will begin to turn golden. Now gradually add the stock, stirring continuously to avoid lumps. As the flour absorbs the stock, the mixture will begin to thicken. When it resembles the thickness of loose mashed potato, stir in the parsley and check the seasoning. Remove from the heat and spread it out on a baking tray. Allow it to cool, then place in the fridge. Once cold, the mixture will firm up and become much easier to form into croquetas.

Shape the mixture into quenelles about the size of a walnut, using 2 large dessertspoons. Heat the oil in a deep-fat fryer or a large saucepan until it reaches about 180°C/350°F, making sure it does not come more than halfway up the sides of the saucepan.

Place the beaten egg and breadcrumbs in separate dishes and dip each croqueta into the egg and then into the breadcrumbs to coat. Fry in the hot oil until crisp and golden all over. Place on kitchen paper to absorb any excess oil. Serve at once.

CRISPY PANCETA, WILD MUSHROOMS AND FINO

This dish is also delicious made with peeled prawns or brown shrimps and
lemon zest instead of the panceta.

Serves 4

8 very thin slices (40g) panceta ibérica or jamón (page 281),
   Italian lardo, pancetta or speck

4 tablespoons olive oil

1-2 garlic cloves, finely chopped

400g fresh chanterelle or porcini mushrooms, or a mixture of
   field and oyster mushrooms, cleaned and thickly sliced

2 tablespoons fino sherry

1 tablespoon finely chopped flat-leaf parsley

4 slices of toast

To crisp the panceta, preheat the oven to 180°C/350°F/Gas 4. Place it on a
rack in the oven for 10-15 minutes until crisp, making sure it doesn't burn.

 Heat the oil in a heavy-based pan over a high heat. When it is hot, but
not smoking, add the garlic. Fry for a few seconds, until the garlic begins
to turn golden, then add the mushrooms and a pinch of salt and continue to
fry for a few minutes, stirring occasionally until soft. Add the fino sherry
and cook for a further minute or so, until a sauce has developed. Stir in
the chopped parsley, check the seasoning and divide the mushrooms between
the slices of toast. Garnish each portion with the crisped panceta and serve
immediately.

CALF'S LIVER, CACIK AND CHILLI BUTTER

Serves 4
300g calf's liver, cut into bite-sized pieces 1.5cm thick
25g butter
1 quantity Chilli Butter (page 116)
paprika, to finish

CACIK
1 small cucumber, peeled and coarsely grated
5 tablespoons strained Greek yoghurt, such as Total
1 garlic clove, crushed to a paste with ½ teaspoon salt
2 tablespoons dill (or mint), shredded, plus extra for
garnish

To make the cacık, gently squeeze the grated cucumber to get rid of excess water, then combine it with the yoghurt, garlic and dill or mint. Add a splash of water if it is too thick and check the seasoning. Set aside.

Season the liver with salt and pepper. Heat a pan over a high heat and add the butter, followed by the liver. Brown the liver on all sides and remove. We generally serve liver still pink in the middle.

Spread the cacık on a plate and scatter the liver on top. Gently warm the chilli butter and pour it over the liver, sprinkle with more dill or mint and a pinch of paprika and serve straight away.

CHICKEN AND PRESERVED LEMON TAGINE

Preserved lemons are found in North Africa, especially Morocco. Whole lemons are pickled in water, lemon juice and salt, with added spices. It takes 1-2 months for the salt to cure the skin before it is ready to use. The pulp of the preserved lemon is used to flavour stews and sauces, but it is the rind that is most valued.

Serves 4
100ml olive oil
2 Spanish onions, finely sliced
4 organic or free-range chicken thighs on the bone, skinless
1 teaspoon cumin seeds, lightly toasted and ground (page 34)
1 tablespoon coriander seeds, ground
15-20 threads of saffron, steeped in 100ml boiling water
a pinch of ground cinnamon
25g preserved lemon rind (page 280), finely chopped
1 garlic clove, finely chopped
¼ teaspoon of ground turmeric
75g pitted green olives
juice of ½ lemon
4 tablespoons finely chopped coriander, plus extra to serve
2 tablespoons roughly chopped roast almonds (optional)

Heat the oil in a saucepan and add the onions with a pinch of salt. Cook for 10 minutes, stirring occasionally, until soft, golden and sweet. Add the chicken together with all the other ingredients except the green olives, lemon juice, half the chopped coriander and the almonds. Season lightly with salt and pepper, as the olives and preserved lemon are salty. Place a lid on the pan and cook over a medium heat for 20-30 minutes, stirring occasionally, until the chicken is tender. Add some water if the sauce becomes too thick.

Stir in the olives and the remaining chopped coriander and cook for a few more minutes. Check the chicken is tender, remove from the heat, and stir in the lemon juice. Scatter the coriander and almonds on top and serve hot.

HARISSA CHICKEN, OLIVES AND PRESERVED LEMON

Serves 4

CHICKEN MARINADE

½ medium onion, finely grated

2 garlic cloves, crushed to a paste with 1 teaspoon salt

½ teaspoon smoked sweet Spanish paprika (page 280)

½ teaspoon ground cinnamon

juice of 1 lemon

1 tablespoon extra virgin olive oil

400g organic or free-range chicken fillets (whole), or breasts sliced into 2cm-thick strips

TO FINISH

50g pitted green olives, roughly chopped

1 tablespoon finely chopped preserved lemon rind (page 280)

juice of ½ lemon

1 tablespoon Harissa (page 176)

2 tablespoons finely chopped coriander, plus a few leaves, to serve

To marinate the chicken, mix the onion, garlic, spices, lemon juice and olive oil in a bowl, add the chicken, coat well and refrigerate for at least 30 minutes or overnight.

The chicken is best charcoal-grilled on a hot barbecue or seared on a griddle pan over a high heat, or under a grill, turning once until just cooked through. Transfer to a bowl, add the olives, preserved lemon, lemon juice, harissa and coriander and mix well. Check the seasoning and serve with extra coriander leaves on top.

CHICKEN, TAHINI YOGHURT AND RED CHILLI

Serves 4

CHICKEN MARINADE

½ small onion, finely grated

2 garlic cloves, crushed to a paste with 1 teaspoon salt

½ teaspoon smoked sweet Spanish paprika (page 280)

½ teaspoon ground cinnamon

juice of 1 lemon

1 tablespoon extra virgin olive oil

400g organic or free-range chicken fillets (whole), or breasts
   sliced into 2cm-thick strips

TAHINI YOGHURT

3 tablespoons tahini

200ml strained Greek yoghurt, such as Total

juice of ½ lemon

2 tablespoons extra virgin olive oil

TO SERVE

1 tablespoon black onion seeds

1 red chilli, deseeded and chopped

a handful of coriander leaves

1 lemon, cut into quarters

Mix the onion, garlic, spices, lemon juice and olive oil in a bowl, add the chicken, coat well and refrigerate for a minimum of 30 minutes or overnight.

The chicken is best charcoal-grilled on a hot barbecue or seared on a griddle pan over a high heat, or under a grill, turning once until just cooked.

To make the tahini yoghurt, put the tahini, yoghurt, lemon juice and olive oil in a bowl, season with salt and pepper and mix well. If the mixture seems too thick, then loosen with a splash of water.

Place the chicken on a plate and spoon the tahini yoghurt over the top. Sprinkle with the black onion seeds, chilli and fresh coriander. Serve with the lemon on the side.

PIRI PIRI CHICKEN

We often get cravings for piri piri chicken. Our first taste of it was working at the Eagle pub together, where chef David Eyre made the most delicious piri piri squid and chicken. This is our version. It makes quite a large amount of the marinade, so some may be kept in the fridge for another occasion. At Morito we never marinate meat for less than 24 hours.

Serves 4

200ml white wine

3 tablespoons Moscatel vinegar (page 280), or a good-quality white wine vinegar with a pinch of sugar

4 small dried red chillies, crumbled

2 teaspoons freshly ground coriander

8 fresh bay leaves, finely chopped

2 Romano peppers (page 280) or 2 small bell peppers

4 large red chillies

2 garlic cloves, crushed to a paste with 1 teaspoon salt

½ teaspoon dried oregano or rosemary

½ teaspoon sugar

⅔ teaspoon smoked hot or sweet Spanish paprika (page 280)

4 tablespoons olive oil

4 organic or free-range chicken drumsticks or 12 wings, skin-on

4 tablespoons very reduced chicken stock (optional)

Place a saucepan over a high heat and add the wine, vinegar, dried chillies, coriander and bay leaves. Boil until the liquid has reduced by half. Turn off the heat and let the flavours infuse.

Next blister the peppers and fresh chillies under a hot grill or over a barbecue or gas flame until the skin is black. When cool enough, peel off the skin and deseed. Combine with the wine reduction and all the remaining ingredients except for the chicken and chicken stock. Blitz in a food processor or liquidiser or with a hand-held blender until smooth. Season.

Trim and score (or prick) the drumsticks or wings, on each side, to help the marinade penetrate beneath the skin. Coat the chicken with 8 tablespoons of the piri piri sauce. Marinate in the fridge for 3-4 hours or overnight.

When you are ready to eat, turn on the grill to a low to medium heat or, preferably, use a barbecue. Grill the chicken on all sides until light brown and slightly crisp. If the meat seems cooked through before it is crisp, turn up the grill a little. You can either serve the chicken with extra piri piri on the side or add it to the reduced chicken stock, if using, and spoon over this spicy gravy.

PIGEON AND MELLOW GARLIC PURÉE

The less you cook garlic the more aggressive the flavour. The longer you cook
it, the mellower it will be. For a more punchy purée, therefore, cook the
garlic in the milk for only 10 minutes. At Morito we also serve this purée
with lamb's kidneys or slivers of salted anchovy and a Morito roll or two.

Serves 4
GARLIC PURÉE
3 heads of new-season garlic, peeled (page 281)
300ml whole milk
1 tablespoon extra virgin olive oil

PIGEON
4 pigeon breasts, or 4 lamb's kidneys
50g butter
½ tablespoon shredded flat-leaf parsley

Place the garlic in a small saucepan and cover with the milk. Simmer for 10
minutes, until the garlic is just soft. Add the olive oil and some salt to
the pan. Using a hand-held blender, purée the garlic with the milk until
smooth. Check the seasoning and keep warm.

If you are using lamb's kidneys, peel off the thin membrane. Slice each
kidney in half lengthways and snip out as much white gristle as possible with
scissors. Then cut each half into bite-sized pieces.

To sear the pigeon breasts or lamb's kidneys, put a frying pan over
a medium to high heat and add the butter. When it begins to foam, season
the pigeon breasts or kidneys well with salt and pepper and add to the pan.
Sear the pigeon for 3-5 minutes on either side, depending on size, until
caramelised. Set aside to relax for a few minutes, then slice, transfer to a
plate and pour over any pan juices. The kidneys require less time - probably
about 3 minutes in total. They should be still pink in the middle. Sprinkle
over the parsley and serve with the warm purée on the side, and some toast.

SLOW-COOKED RABBIT

This is a very moreish rabbit stew with subtle hints of rosemary and orange.

Serves 6-8
1 rabbit (1-1.2kg), cut into 8 pieces
200ml olive oil
400ml red wine
8 red onions, sliced
1 leek, sliced
5 carrots, sliced
2 teaspoons dried oregano
8 bay leaves, preferably fresh
4 sprigs of thyme
4 sprigs of rosemary
3 large (2cm x 3cm) strips of orange zest
2 cinnamon sticks
2 teaspoons ground allspice
500g tomato passata or tomato purée
1-2 tablespoons Forum Cabernet Sauvignon vinegar (page 280), or
 a good-quality aged red wine vinegar with a pinch of sugar

Season the rabbit pieces well with salt and pepper. Heat the olive oil in a
large pan, add the rabbit and cook over a high heat for a few minutes until it
begins to colour on both sides. Add the red wine and cook for 2 more minutes.
Add the onions, leek and carrots to the pan together with the oregano, bay
leaves, thyme, rosemary, orange zest and spices. Continue to cook until the
onions begin to soften a little. Add the tomato passata or purée, check the
seasoning, then lower the heat to medium and cook gently for 30-40 minutes or
until the rabbit is tender and almost falling off the bone. Add the splash of
vinegar, give the stew a good stir and remove from the heat. Serve hot, along
with a crisp green salad and a cold beer, or with a chilled glass of red wine.

MORITO

PUDDINGS

Puddings

We do not have an extensive repertoire of puddings at Morito, just something on offer to satisfy a sweet tooth.

CREMA CATALANA

The scent of citrus permeates the custard in a subtle and classy way.

> Serves 8
> 1 litre whole milk
> zest of 1 orange, peeled off in 1.5cm-wide strips
> zest of 1 lemon, peeled off in 1.5cm-wide strips
> 1 cinnamon stick
> 1 vanilla pod, split lengthways
> 15 organic or free-range egg yolks
> 190g caster sugar, plus 8 tablespoons to serve
> 20g cornflour

Place the milk, citrus zest, cinnamon stick and vanilla pod in a saucepan and gently bring to the boil. Remove from the heat and allow to infuse for 15 minutes.

Meanwhile, whisk the egg yolks with the 190g sugar and the cornflour until pale and creamy. Pass the milk through a sieve and discard the aromatics. Return the milk to the saucepan and place over a medium heat. Add the egg mixture and whisk continuously for 6-8 minutes until it begins to thicken. When it is thick enough to coat the back of a wooden spoon, remove from the heat and pour into individual bowls or ramekins. Cover the custards with discs of baking parchment to prevent a skin developing. Leave to cool before refrigerating.

To serve, sprinkle 1 tablespoon of sugar on top of each custard and caramelise using a blowtorch. If you do not own a blowtorch, place the sugared custards on a baking tray, and leave under a preheated grill for a few minutes until the sugar turns dark brown. Allow the sugar to harden, then serve immediately.

WALNUT BAKLAVA

When Morito first opened, we used to buy baklava from Antepliler on Green Lanes, as it is some of the best in London. We now make our own.

Serves 8–10

FILLING
- 450g walnuts
- 70g caster sugar
- 1 teaspoon ground cinnamon
- a pinch of ground cloves
- finely grated zest of 2 oranges
- 2 tablespoons white breadcrumbs

SYRUP
- 350g caster sugar
- 1 cinnamon stick
- 10 cardamom pods, lightly crushed
- zest of 1 lemon
- zest of 1 orange
- 450ml water
- ½ tablespoon dried rose petals (page 280) (optional)
- 4 tablespoons rosewater

TO ASSEMBLE
- 250g salted butter
- 350g filo pastry sheets
- dried rose petals or finely chopped pistachios, to serve (optional)

Blitz the walnuts in a food processor until they resemble breadcrumbs. Transfer to a bowl, mix in the remaining filling ingredients and set aside.

Place all the syrup ingredients except the rosewater in a pan. Gently bring to the boil and simmer until the syrup has thickened and coats the back of a spoon lightly (like single cream). This should take around 30 minutes. Remove from the heat, stir in the rosewater and leave to cool.

Preheat the oven to 160°C/325°F/Gas 3. Melt the butter and begin to layer the baklava. We use a round tin about 25cm in diameter or a rectangular baking tray. Brush the tin or tray with butter and line with a sheet of filo. You want the pastry to come up the sides a little. If the filo sheets are too large, you may wish to cut them to fit your tray. Brush the sheet of filo with butter and repeat this process until you have placed 7 sheets of filo in the tray, making sure that each layer is generously buttered. Add half the walnut mixture and then top with another 3 buttered filo sheets. Add the remaining walnut mixture and add another 7 layers of filo, buttering each one as you go. When you have finished, seal the loose ends by tucking the top layers of filo down the sides to meet the bottom ones. Using a sharp knife, score the pastry into diamonds. Bake for approximately 1 hour, until golden and crisp.

Remove the baklava from the oven and pour the cold syrup all over. It may seem like a large quantity of syrup, but it will slowly be absorbed by the baklava as it cools down. Scatter with some rose petals or chopped pistachios, if you wish. Baklava is delicious served warm, with a scoop of Vanilla Ice Cream (page 260) or a small cup of coffee.

WALNUT CAKE

This cake is delicious with a small glass of sweet or medium Oloroso or Pedro Ximénez sherry (page 281).

Serves 8
150g unsalted butter, at room temperature
300g caster sugar
150ml sunflower oil
6 organic or free-range eggs, separated
finely grated zest and juice of 1 lemon
½ teaspoon ground cinnamon
1 whole nutmeg, grated
100g coarse polenta
100g self-raising flour
½ teaspoon baking powder
½ teaspoon bicarbonate of soda
250g walnuts, roughly chopped
100g ground almonds

Preheat the oven to 180°C/350°F/Gas 4. Line a 20-25cm round cake tin with baking parchment.

Whisk the butter in an electric mixer fitted with a balloon whisk for 10 minutes, until pale and fluffy. Add the sugar and continue to whisk for 15 minutes, until even paler and fluffier. With the mixer still running, slowly add the sunflower oil, followed by the egg yolks, one by one, then the lemon zest and juice.

Mix all the dry ingredients together, including the walnuts and almonds, and fold them into the egg mixture. Whisk the egg whites in a separate bowl until they form soft peaks, then gently fold them into the cake batter.

Pour the mixture into the prepared tin and bake for approximately 1 hour 20 minutes, or until a skewer inserted into the centre of the cake comes out clean. Remove from the oven and leave to cool on a wire rack.

MARIANNA'S GRAPE COMPÔTE

When Marianna decribed this recipe that she ate when she was growing up in Crete, it sounded perfect for Morito, and it was; quick to make, light and extremely Moorish.

> **Serves 4-6**
> **500g sultana grapes or Muscat grapes**
> **250g caster sugar**
> **a splash of water**
> **juice of 1 lemon**
> **400-500g strained Greek yoghurt such as Total, or Labneh**
>   **(page 91), to serve**

Wash the grapes and transfer to a heavy-based saucepan together with the sugar and water. Over a low heat, gently simmer the grapes, stirring occasionally, for 45 minutes to 1 hour or until a syrup has developed and is thick enough to coat the back of a spoon and the grapes are dark brown in colour. Stir in the lemon juice and remove from the heat. Allow to cool. Serve with the yoghurt or labneh. Any excess can be stored in a sterilised jar in the fridge for up to a week.

VANILLA ICE CREAM

A simple vanilla ice cream is a wonderful base for all manner of variations. At Morito, we often serve it *affogato* style with a shot of espresso poured over the top. The variations that follow are also delicious.

Makes 1 litre
500ml double cream
250ml whole milk
½ cinnamon stick
½ vanilla pod, split lengthways
8 organic or free-range egg yolks
85g caster sugar

Put the cream, milk, cinnamon and vanilla pod in a saucepan and gently bring to the boil. Remove from the heat, discard the cinnamon stick and vanilla pod and set aside. Using an electric mixer, whisk the egg yolks and sugar for 10 minutes, until pale and stiff. Whisk the egg mixture into the cream mixture and return to a low heat, whisking continuously. After a few minutes the mixture will begin to thicken; remove from the heat and place the saucepan in a sink or bowl of cold water and ice to cool down quickly.

If using an ice cream machine, follow the manufacturer's instructions to churn the mixture. If you do not have a machine, place the custard in a shallow container in the freezer and whisk it briefly every 30 minutes for 2 hours in order to break down any crystals that may form. Leave the ice cream in the freezer overnight if possible. If it feels too hard the next day, remove it from the freezer 15 minutes before serving.

COFFEE ICE CREAM

Reduce the amount of milk in the vanilla ice cream (opposite) by 100ml and replace with 100ml espresso, adding the cooled coffee after the cream and milk come off the heat.

PX ICE CREAM

Soak 150g sultanas or raisins in 200ml Pedro Ximénez sherry (page 281) until plump. It helps to warm the sherry slightly. Drain off the excess sherry and set aside. Stir the raisins into the vanilla ice cream (opposite) before churning. Pour the leftover sherry over the ice cream as you serve.

AMARETTO AND SALTED MARCONA ALMOND ICE CREAM

Add 70ml amaretto to the vanilla ice cream (opposite) when you remove the pan from the heat. Sprinkle with 2 tablespoons crushed salted Marcona almonds (page 281) before serving.

ANISE BISCUITS

A perfect biscuit for ice cream.

Makes 15-20 biscuits
150g plain flour
25g semolina
1½ teaspoons green aniseed (page 280), lightly crushed
110g unsalted butter
50g caster sugar

Sift the flour into a bowl and add the semolina and aniseed. Melt the butter and mix with the sugar, then fold into the flour mix and work the mixture with your hands until it becomes a soft dough. Roll it into a cylinder, wrap in cling film and refrigerate for at least 1 hour.

Preheat the oven to 190°C/375°F/Gas 5. Remove the biscuit dough from the fridge, unwrap and cut into 1cm-thick discs. Place them on a baking tray lined with baking parchment and bake for 15-20 minutes, until golden brown. Remove from the oven and leave to cool.

DRINKS

Drinks

One of the first things to strike any visitor to Morito is how small the space is - compact, cosy, bijou or cramped, depending on your perspective. From the beginning, it was apparent that this was a fact that would, by necessity, influence how we went about our business. With very little space behind the bar, the drinks on offer were always going to be limited and initially, at least, the cocktail list was no exception. We started with just Rebujito and Cava Pomegranate but over time, in a very natural and unforced manner, it's grown and matured nicely - as we hope we have too.

A NOTE ON MEASURES

At Morito, compelled as we are to keep track of our stock, we use measures to make all of the following drinks. In the knowledge that most people don't have a range of spirit jiggers at home, in the first two sections we have just given proportions and left the exact quantities to your discretion. The third selection of drinks requires a little more precision and, in some cases, a cocktail shaker – an investment well worth making, we suggest. Happy mixing and drinking!

Spritzer-type drinks

REBUJITO

Every year in Jerez there is a *feria*, a civic celebration of sherry on a massive scale. Imagine a combination of music festival and village fête at which almost every stall or stage is a sherry bar of one kind or another. This was the setting for Moro's fifteenth-anniversary staff knees-up and for many of us an unforgettable and intoxicating introduction to the Rebujito. It is a fantastic summer drink - cool, refreshing and delicious. At Morito we mix them individually, but there's no reason why you can't make up big jugs for a barbecue, picnic or party.

> 1 part fino sherry to 1 part lemonade, Sprite or La Casera (page 281). Add mint leaves and ice and you're there.

La Casera is a Spanish soft drink and is quite tricky to get hold of, but you can approximate it by mixing ordinary lemonade and soda water in equal quantities.

It helps to release the flavour of the mint leaves if you rip them, but this means bits in the drink. Instead, try holding the mint in your hands and clapping theatrically. It's fun. We use Tio Pepe, but any dry fino will do. If you are mixing in large quantities, don't worry about the lemonade going flat - they don't in Jerez!

CAVA POMEGRANATE

This simple but sexy cava cocktail is a real crowd-pleaser. Whether you attribute this to the reputation of pomegranate as an antioxidant-packed super-food or to the simple allure of pink, fizzy booze is perhaps a moot point. Either way it's a lovely drink.

| **2 parts cava to 1 part pomegranate juice (ideally fresh).**

At Morito we garnish this drink with a pomegranate juice ice cube with a single pomegranate seed frozen in the middle - a nice but purely cosmetic touch.

TINTO DE VERANO

As a tourist in Andalucía, it's hard to escape sangria, but the locals prefer its simplified cousin, tinto de verano, or 'wine of summer'. Don't use expensive wine for this - go for something fruity and non-tannic. La Casera is a Spanish soft drink and is quite tricky to get hold of, but you can approximate it by mixing ordinary lemonade and soda water in equal quantities.

| **3 parts red wine to 1 part lemonade or La Casera (page 281).**
| **Pour over ice and add orange and/or lemon slices.**

PORTONIC

An occasional perk of the restaurant business is being taken by our suppliers to visit wineries and vineyards. On a recent jaunt to Portugal, Moro waiter Jason Starmer came back raving about an aperitif he'd been served at a Porto hotel. Within days it was on the list. Whatever you do, don't confuse dry white port with ruby or tawny port.

| **1 part dry white port to 3 parts tonic water. Pour over ice**
| **and add a lime and/or lemon slice.**

Vermouth and Campari, a bittersweet love affair

One day a sample bottle of a Spanish vermouth arrived with our house wine delivery. The label was effortlessly cool in a retro kind of way and when we tried it and found it to be utterly delicious we immediately set about mixing it with pretty much anything. Before long, it was integral to our ever-expanding list and, of course, you can't have vermouth without Campari, so we started ordering that too...

VERMUT ESPUMOSO

This really is a classy affair - you may be sweating from the Tube, stressed after a hard day's work and contemplating the cramped confines of a rented room, but mix yourself one of these and you'll be transported to Madrid in the Jazz Age. Maybe.

> **1 part Lacuesta Vermut Rojo (page 281) to 2 parts cava. Pour over ice and add a slice of orange.**

If you can't track down Lacuesta Vermut then use any premium-quality sweet vermouth. Martini Rosso doesn't really cut the mustard in this instance.

FINO LACUESTA

Even more sophisticated than the Espumoso (above) - this time you're on a yacht or something.

> **2 parts fino or manzanilla sherry to 1 part Lacuesta Vermut Rojo (page 281). Pour over ice, add a couple of drops of orange bitters (page 281) and garnish with orange peel.**

We use a standard vegetable peeler to pare oranges and lemons. Always do this last and directly over the drink and then squeeze the peel between your fingers so you get as much pungent citrus oil as possible. You can then roll up the peel to make a twist or just drop it in as it is. The bitters are not essential but they do add a certain something.

NEGRONI

It's verging on cheeky to list a recipe for this, as it's such a classic, but what the hell. Using Spanish Lacuesta Vermut Rojo and our wonderfully aromatic Xoriguer gin from Menorca means we probably get away with it.

> **Equal parts Lacuesta Vermut Rojo (page 281), Xoriguer gin (page 281) and Campari. Pour over ice, add a couple of drops of orange bitters (page 281) (optional) and garnish with orange and lemon peel.**

The orange bitters are pretty controversial so leave them out if you prefer, but we like them.

NEGRONI AMONTILLADO

Paul 'Shooter' McGough arrived from Tasmania in late 2011. With his bushy orange beard and fondness for loud shirts and funky music, he had surely found his natural home at Morito, but he was snaffled up by the Moro bar and restricted to the odd guest appearance with us. However, he did contribute some awesome drinks and this is one of them. To purists, it probably sounds plain wrong, but the deep, nutty tones of the amontillado harmonise nicely with the herby bitterness of the Campari and vermouth.

> **2 parts amontillado sherry to 1 part Lacuesta Vermut Rojo (page 281) and 1 part Campari. Pour over ice and garnish with orange peel.**

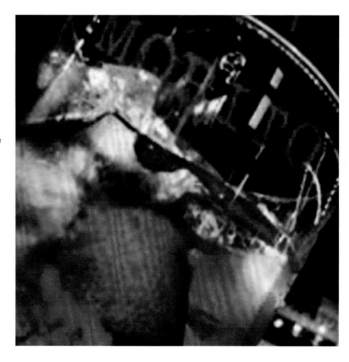

BICICLETA

This is another classic, but it's well worth reminding yourself what a great combo it is - just a brilliant, brilliant drink. You'd have to be mad not to love it - or someone who doesn't like Campari or white wine, or getting drunk as the sun sets, or talking about European cinema. The wine should be crisp and not overly rich or oaky.

> 1 part Campari and 2 or 3 parts white wine (experiment and see what you prefer). Pour over ice and add a slice of orange.

'Others'

GINTONIC

It might sound absurd to list a gin and tonic as a cocktail but the difference between a measly 25ml measure with half-melted ice, flat tonic and a sad slice of lemon from your local pub, and the majestic drink that you will be served in many parts of Spain is reason enough.

> **70ml Xoriguer gin (page 281)**
> **125ml tonic water**
> **lemon zest**

You need to fill the glass with ice - fresh ice, ice that isn't going to melt immediately and dilute your drink. You need to be liberal with the gin and sparing with the tonic. Finally, you need to embrace the peeler as the tool to prepare your garnish. Having mixed your drink, hold the lemon directly over the glass and peel 3 strips of peel into it. The difference between the delicate but powerful citrus aroma you get this way, as opposed to the slight bitterness of squeezed juice or the negligible impact of a slice, dropped in as an afterthought, is amazing. For maximum zest, squeeze each bit of peel between your fingers before you drop it in. At Dickens bar in San Sebastian (where a Gintonic costs 12 euros and is worth every cent) they scrape two bits of peel against one another over the drink with extraordinary focus and dedication.

BLOODY OLD-FASHIONED

Another one of Paul McGough's (see his negroni on page 270). This was born out of a desire to get people drinking bourbon, because before we put this on the list we couldn't shift it for love nor money. It's a twist on the classic Old-Fashioned and it's delicious. Blood oranges have a very limited season so you can use ordinary oranges, if necessary.

50ml bourbon
50ml freshly squeezed blood orange juice
a few drops of Angostura bitters and orange bitters (page 281)
a splash of Sugar Syrup (page 277)
a slice of blood orange

Mix all the ingredients except the orange slice in a heavy-bottomed glass or cocktail shaker full of ice. Stir well and then strain into a rocks glass full of ice. Garnish with the slice of blood orange.

PX ESPRESSO MARTINI

Dark, luxurious, rich, complex - this is like coffee, dessert and digestif
all rolled into one.

50ml vodka
35ml Pedro Ximénez sherry (page 281)
35ml espresso
3 coffee beans

You need a cocktail shaker for this one, filled with ice, and you need to
shake all the ingredients except the coffee beans in it long and hard for
at least 20 seconds. Strain into a chilled glass. The shaking will create
the emulsification that gives this drink such an eye-catching appearance -
an off-white *crema* that supports the coffee beans and contrasts nicely with
the darker tones of the rest of the drink. It's important that you add the
coffee last when mixing the drink because if you add it first, it will melt
the ice and dilute the drink. If you don't have a home espresso machine, you
can use any coffee as long as it's very, very strong... As an even simpler
alternative, just add some PX sherry to ordinary filter coffee and pour over
ice - you could add some milk or cream if you like, too.

Moorish-infused cocktails and spirits

SEVILLE ORANGE GIN MARTINI

This very dry gin martini combines orange in many different forms and results in a delicious aperitif.

> 70ml Seville-orange-infused Gin (below)
> 10ml Cointreau
> 2 or 3 drops of orange bitters (page 281)
> 3 drops of orange blossom water (page 280)
> a large piece of orange zest

Chill a martini glass with a scoop of ice. Combine the gin, Cointreau, bitters and orange blossom water in a Boston shaker. Add a large scoop of ice and stir gently until nice and cold. Strain into the emptied martini glass. Twist the orange zest over the drink, ensuring the orange oil sprays in.

SEVILLE-ORANGE-INFUSED GIN

Any gin can be used for this, as most of the flavour comes from the oranges.

> Makes 1 litre
> 1 litre gin
> zest of 5 Seville oranges (available in early January)
>   (page 281), or other thick-skinned oranges like blood
>   oranges, removed in thin strips

Empty a small amount of gin from the bottle to make room for the zest and then put all the zest into the bottle. Using the small amount of gin taken from the bottle, make yourself a gin and tonic to reward yourself for your hard work.

   Leave the Seville gin for at least one month to infuse. Strain through a muslin cloth and re-bottle.

MORITOPOLITAN

A dramatic twist on the classic Cosmopolitan, this cocktail is very much like
a liquid Turkish Delight.

> 70ml Barberry Vodka (below)
> 10ml Cointreau
> 35ml pomegranate juice
> ½ teaspoon pomegranate molasses (page 280)
> ½ teaspoon Sugar Syrup (opposite)
> a dash of lemon juice (about 10ml)
> 6 drops of rosewater (page 280)
> 6-7 rose petals (page 280)

Chill a martini glass with a scoop of ice. Combine all the ingredients except
the rose petals in a Boston shaker. Add a scoop of ice, shake vigorously and
strain into the emptied martini glass. Garnish with rose petals.

BARBERRY VODKA

> Makes 1 litre
> 1 litre vodka (we use Stolichnaya, but any vodka will be fine)
> 100g dried barberries (page 280)

Pour enough vodka out of the bottle to make room for the berries. Roughly
chop the barberries and put them into the vodka bottle. Leave for one month.
Strain through a sieve, then through a muslin cloth. Re-bottle and enjoy.

COSITA DE MANZANA (THE APPLE THING)

Amazingly aromatic and complex, but a surprisingly refreshing combination
of flavours.

> 70ml Cardamom Vodka (opposite)
> 10ml Sugar Syrup (opposite)
> juice of ½ lime, plus a lime wedge to serve
> 35ml cloudy apple juice

Combine all the ingredients except the lime wedge in a Boston shaker. Add
2 scoops of ice and shake vigorously. Strain over 1 scoop of ice in a rocks
glass, then garnish with the lime wedge. Sit down and enjoy.

CARDAMOM VODKA

Makes 1 litre
20 green cardamom pods
1 litre vodka (we use Stolichnaya, but any vodka will be fine)

Place the cardamom pods in the vodka bottle and leave for two weeks to infuse. Strain the vodka to remove the pods (if left for longer, the flavour will become too strong) and re-bottle.

SUGAR SYRUP

Put 500g caster sugar in a heavy-based saucepan and just cover with water. Place over a medium-low heat to allow the sugar to dissolve in the water. Once clear, bring to a gentle simmer, then boil until reduced, thick and syrupy. Pour into a sterilised bottle.

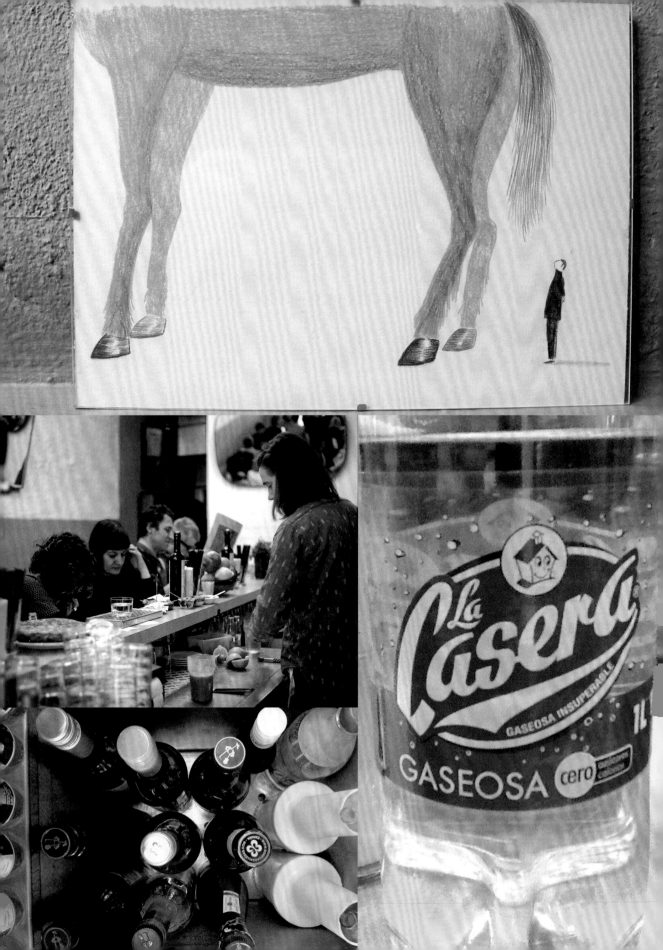

SUPPLIERS

Most of these more
unusual ingredients
can be bought online.

SPICES
Aleppo chilli flakes
www.ottolenghi.co.uk
www.thespicery.com

baharat
www.ottolenghi.co.uk
www.thespicery.com

barberries
www.foratasteofpersia.
  co.uk
www.ottolenghi.co.uk

**black cumin seeds (kala
jeera)**
www.theasiancookshop.
  co.uk

**black onion/nigella
seeds**
www.ottolenghi.co.uk
www.thespicery.com

green aniseed
www.ottolenghi.co.uk
www.thespicery.com

**paprika, smoked (hot and
sweet)**
www.brindisa.com
www.thespicery.com

**paprika, unsmoked (hot
and sweet)**
www.thespicery.com

rose petals (dried)
www.foratasteofpersia.
  co.uk
www.thespicery.com

sumac
www.ottolenghi.co.uk
www.thespicery.com

za'atar
www.ottolenghi.co.uk
www.thespicery.com

VINEGARS, OILS,
MOLASSES, BLOSSOM
WATERS AND SAUCES
argan oil
www.ottolenghi.co.uk
www.wildwoodgroves.com

date molasses
www.ottolenghi.co.uk

**Forum Cabernet Sauvignon
vinegar**
www.brindisa.com

harissa
www.belazu.com
www.thespicery.com

**miel de caña (cane
molasses)**
www.saborear.co.uk

Moscatel vinegar
www.brindisa.com
www.ottolenghi.co.uk

olive oil
www.basilippo.com

orange blossom water
www.ottolenghi.co.uk
www.waitrose.com

pomegranate molasses
www.ottolenghi.co.uk
www.souschef.co.uk

rosewater
www.ottolenghi.co.uk
www.waitrose.com

sherry vinegar
www.brindisa.com
www.ottolenghi.co.uk

verjus
www.souschef.co.uk

OLIVES AND PICKLES
caper berries
www.brindisa.com
www.ultracomida.co.uk

capers in brine
www.waitrose.com

olives
www.fresholive.com
www.waitrose.com

preserved lemon
www.belazu.com
www.waitrose.com

**Spanish pickled chillies
(guindilla)**
www.brindisa.com

Turkish pickled chillies
www.marketurk.com

PEPPERS
**green peppers
(frigitelli)**
www.natoora.co.uk
www.waitrose.com

guindillas (dried)
www.brindisa.com
www.melburyandappleton.
  co.uk

ñoras (dried)
www.brindisa.com
www.melburyandappleton.
  co.uk

padrón peppers
www.brindisa.com
www.waitrose.com

piquillo peppers
www.brindisa.com

**preserved cherry
chillies (pepperdew)**
www.fresholive.com
www.waitrose.com

Romano peppers
www.waitrose.com

OTHER VEGETABLES AND
FRUIT
bergamot orange
www.natoora.co.uk

black radish
www.natoora.co.uk

new-season garlic
www.natoora.co.uk
www.thegarlicfarm.co.uk

purslane
www.natoora.co.uk

Seville orange
www.natoora.co.uk

white daikon (mooli)
www.natoora.co.uk

FISH
boquerones
www.brindisa.com

North Atlantic shell-on prawns
www.thefishsociety.co.uk

octopus
www.thefishsociety.co.uk

Ortiz salted anchovies and tuna
www.brindisa.com

Palamos red prawns
www.iberflavours.com

puntillitas/baby squid
www.thefishsociety.co.uk

salt cod
www.brindisa.com
www.thefishsociety.co.uk

sea urchin roe
www.thefishsociety.co.uk

squid ink
www.rgarciaandsons.com
www.souschef.co.uk
www.thefishsociety.co.uk

CURED MEATS
butifarra
www.iberflavours.com
www.melburyandappleton.
 co.uk

cecina
www.ultracomida.co.uk

chorizo (cooking and slicing)
www.brindisa.com

jamón ibérico
www.bartozino.com
www.brindisa.com

morcilla
www.brindisa.com

panceta
www.brindisa.com

sausage stuffing
www.naturalsausageskins.
 co.uk

MISCELLANEOUS
chickpeas (in jars)
www.brindisa.com
www.ultracomida.co.uk
(listed as Garbanzos)

crisps (Spanish olive oil)
www.lafromagerie.com
www.rgarciaandsons.com
www.waitrose.com
(selected stores)

dried fava beans
www.melburyandappleton.
 co.uk
www.souschef.co.uk

fideos
www.rgarciaandsons.com
www.saborear.co.uk

fresh goat's cheese
www.waitrose.com

frying flour for fish
www.rgarciaandsons.com

garlic shoots/ajetes (in jars)
www.ultracomida.co.uk

goat's curd
www.nealsyarddairy.co.uk

membrillo (quince cheese)
www.brindisa.com

paella rice
www.brindisa.com
www.rgarciaandsons.com

picos breadsticks
www.ultracomida.co.uk

Picos de Europa cheese
www.brindisa.com

polenta
www.waitrose.com

roasted Marcona almonds
www.brindisa.com

rock salt (Tidman's/ Maldon)
www.waitrose.com

tetilla cheese
www.brindisa.com

warka/feuilles de Brick
www.frenchclick.co.uk

DRINKS
bitters
www.amathusdrinks.com

La Casera
www.rgarciaandsons.com

Lacuesta Vermut Rojo
www.albionwineshippers.
 co.uk

sherry
www.albionwineshippers.
 co.uk
www.corneyandbarrow.com
www.leaandsandeman.co.uk
www.waitrose.com

Xoriguer gin
www.amathusdrinks.com

INDEX

1 3 5 7 9 10 8 6 4 2

Published in 2014 by Ebury Press, an imprint of
Ebury Publishing

A Random House Group Company

Text © Sam and Sam Clark 2014
Photography © Ebury Press 2014
Rita Hayworth as Gilda (p.39) © Mary Evans
Picture Library

Sam and Sam Clark have asserted their right
to be identified as the authors of this Work
in accordance with the Copyright, Designs and
Patents Act 1988

The Random House Group Limited Reg. No. 954009

Addresses for companies within the Random House
Group can be found at www.randomhouse.co.uk

A CIP catalogue record for this book is available
from the British Library

The Random House Group Limited supports the
Forest Stewardship Council® (FSC®), the leading
international forest-certification organisation.
Our books carrying the FSC label are printed
on FSC®-certified paper. FSC is the only
forest-certification scheme supported by the
leading environmental organisations, including
Greenpeace. Our paper procurement policy can be
found at www.randomhouse.co.uk/environment

To buy books by your favourite authors and
register for offers visit www.randomhouse.co.uk

Design: Caz Hildebrand/heredesign.co.uk
Photography: Toby Glanville, Elliot Sheppard and
the Morito team
Project editor: Laura Herring

Printed and bound in Italy by Graphicom SRL
Colour origination by Altaimage, London

ISBN: 9780091947309

MIX
Paper from
responsible sources
FSC® C013123

For Ivo

Ebury Press: Sam and I would like to thank our wonderful publisher Ebury Press: **Fiona MacIntyre** for her invaluable wisdom and belief in the project and for giving up so much of her precious time to work with us. Our editor **Laura Herring** for being so supportive, hard-working and patient throughout. Production Director **Helen Everson** must be thanked for the quality of the production on what must have been a very tricky book and to **Sarah Bennie** and **Di Riley** for their invaluable support with the all-important PR.

PR: the brilliant **Mark Hutchinson** has been behind the project since it was first conceived. He and colleague **Kirsten Dennis** have helped build Morito's modest profile in a gradual and natural way with gentle guidance and wisdom.

Additional edits: Sarah Barlow and **Jane Middleton** have been absolutely indispensable in proofing the text with their perfectionism and meticulous attention to detail.

Book design: Caz Hildebrand of **Here Design** remains our rock and our friend, pulling out the strokes of genius just at the right time to move the design along, and to **Mark Paton** and **Kate Marlow** for providing a desk in the Here office for 3 months! **www.heredesign.co.uk**

Team Morito: this book is nothing without Team Morito: founding manager **Hugo Thurston** has been such a positive force and support on every level, and here most notably in the drinks chapter. We are blessed with such an amazing, close-knit team: everyone past and present, in the kitchen, bar and on the floor, must be thanked as all have contributed to how Morito has been moulded and evolved over the last 3 years. And also to everyone at Moro as the two are joined at the hip.

Kitchen: head chef **Marianna Leivaditaki** has been by our side, helping test and write recipes and take photographs. Her work was really important to the whole project. We can't thank her enough, and to **Henry Russell**, who is at the helm in the Morito kitchen, helping us take the food to new and exciting levels.

Photography: the photography for this book was teamwork over the course of 2 years, as chefs, waiters and managers were encouraged to snap away on their phones, most notably **Sasha Scott**, **Josie Martin**, **Tabitha Money**, **Simon Money** and **Maxi Smith**. The result was a lot of images, not all good, but the occasional gem. We gratefully accepted the help of our head barman and photographer **Elliot Sheppard**, who upped the quality crucially and considerably. We also enlisted our friend and photographer **Toby Glanville**, who we worked with on *Moro East*, to collaborate with us once again and scatter his magic and calm through the pages. **www.tobyglanville.com**

Design of Morito: Genevieve Murray is the architect behind Morito, and she and the wonderful artist **Dillwyn Smith** have been instrumental in the look of Morito since it was first conceived. Dillwyn tirelessly sourced furniture, chose finishes and refined our colours. In addition to this, he also produced the amazing tiled piece that surrounds the bar, a detail of which is the Morito cover. **www.dillwynsmith.com**